KU-506-539

WITHDRAWN

THE LEARNING CENTRE
HAMMERSMITH AND WEST
LONDON COLLEGE
GLIDDON ROAD
LONDON W14 9BL

Instant MBA

HAMMERSMITH WEST LONDON COLLEGE

336653

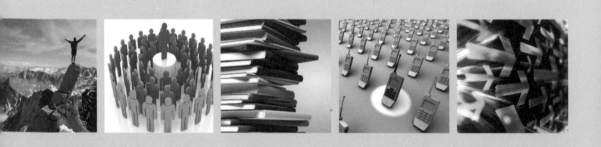

Instant
MBA

Think, perform and earn like a
top business-school graduate

Nicholas Bate

brilliantideas

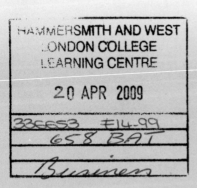

HAMMERSMITH AND WEST
LONDON COLLEGE
LEARNING CENTRE

20 APR 2009

336653   £14.99
658 BAT

Business

Careful now

More and more organisations are
demanding MBA-level thinking from
people across a broad spectrum of roles
and specialisms; more and more people
are looking for a career boost which
can take them to the next stage or into
the world of successful self-
employment.

A formal MBA might seem to provide a
convenient solution, but it's not the
ticket to fabulous fortune that it once
was. Learning to think in an MBA way,
however, can really help you – and this
book might well aid you on your way.
But you have to be willing to put in the
work yourself, of course. We'd love to,
but we can't hold your hand all the
time or guarantee you the
advancement you hope for – nor, it has
to be said, are we responsible for the
consequences of any actions you might
choose to take. Think about what you
do and how you set about doing it, and
you should reap the benefits.

Now, the Internet is a great resource
for anyone studying an MBA, whether
an Instant MBA or a more formal one.
However, there are both good and bad
sources of information online and the
web is a constantly changing
phenomenon. Be circumspect and bear
in mind that websites change, so if you
can't find the recommended blog by a
particular business guru, do a search to
find its new home.

Copyright © Infinite Ideas Limited, 2008
The right of Nicholas Bate to be identified as the author of this book has been
asserted in accordance with the Copyright, Designs and Patents Act 1988.

First published in 2008 by
Infinite Ideas Limited
36 St Giles
Oxford, OX1 3LD
United Kingdom
www.infideas.com

All rights reserved. Except for the quotation of small passages for the purposes
of criticism or review, no part of this publication may be reproduced, stored in
a retrieval system or transmitted in any form or by any means, electronic,
mechanical, photocopying, recording, scanning or otherwise, except under the
terms of the Copyright, Designs and Patents Act 1988 or under the terms of a
licence issued by the Copyright Licensing Agency Ltd, 90 Tottenham Court
Road, London W1T 4LP, UK, without the permission in writing of the publisher.
Requests to the publisher should be addressed to the Permissions Department,
Infinite Ideas Limited, 36 St Giles, Oxford, OX1 3LD, UK, or faxed to +44 (0)1865
514777.

A CIP catalogue record for this book is available from the British Library

ISBN 978–1–905940–83–7

Brand and product names are trademarks or registered trademarks of their
respective owners.

Designed and typeset by Baseline Arts Ltd, Oxford
Printed in India

336653

Brilliant ideas

Brilliant features

Each chapter of this book is designed to provide you with an inspirational idea that you can read quickly and put into practice straight away.

Throughout you'll find three features that will help you get right to the heart of the idea:

- *Here's an idea for you* Take it on board and give it a go – right here, right now. Get an idea of how well you're doing so far.

- *Defining idea* Words of wisdom from masters and mistresses of the art, plus some interesting hangers-on.

- *How did it go?* If at first you do succeed, try to hide your amazement. If, on the other hand, you don't, then this is where you'll find a Q and A that highlights common problems and how to get over them.

Introduction

So: the MBA. Those magical three letters – rapid promotion, a better job with a decent car and untold wealth! Well, maybe. All of these things can happen and do happen. The only challenge is that it's a big investment to take a year out of your career path or commit endless weekends to a part-time version. Especially when what you really want is to be able to think, perform and, hopefully, earn like a top MBA student.

That's what this book is designed to do: give you MBA thinking without the MBA schedule of assignments; give you the MBA language and models without wading through the endless reading lists of textbooks. To give your brain a refresh. And, incidentally, if you are already doing your MBA it'll help you distinguish what's vital from what's trivial, too.

You're smart and ambitious and want an accelerator, or you're a bit jaded and you want to reinvent your career. Either way this book will help – because, as you are probably aware, the MBA is shifting ever so, ever so slightly. Of course the old favourites, such as Boston Matrices or Porter's value chain, are still there. But the new MBAs are fighting hard to win time on softer skills – emotional intelligence and experiential marketing, for example. That's what your current employer needs now (in fact, craves now) or is what your future employer will want to be convinced – at the interview – that you can offer. Here's the point which is often lost: however much you study some MBA topics, few people get the chance to influence them hugely. But with experiential marketing or personal leadership – well, it's down to you and that's very exciting!

So, this book covers the essentials of all the classic MBA areas such as Gary Hamel's ideas about core competency. This will ensure you understand their relevance and can talk intelligently about the concept concerned. But, perhaps more importantly, it also considers the rapidly emerging areas of the new, softer MBA; aspects such as emotional intelligence and inspirational leadership. These have a little more emphasis.

What will the book do for you?
- Get you thinking again.
- Get you thinking radically.
- Get you thinking critically.
- Introduce you to some brilliant business models.
- Get you working on your business.
- Get you ahead of the game.
- Ensure you are an attractive candidate at interviews.
- Give you fewer of the ideas you can't personally influence.
- Give you lots of the ideas you can personally influence.
- Get you to realise that the MBA can be more of a mindset than a qualification, an action plan rather than a sterile text, a source of inspiration rather than an 'I ought to have one of those'.

And much, much more…

You'll learn how to:
- Create an amazing value chain for your business (brilliant idea 2).
- Start a revolution (brilliant idea 8).

- Understand the New World of Work (brilliant idea: lots!).
- Be an entrepreneur (brilliant idea 38).
- Start a blog (brilliant idea 46).

You'll be surprised that:
- Communication is better without PowerPoint a lot of the time (brilliant idea 4).
- Pricing is not about cost (brilliant idea 11).
- Storytelling is where it's at (brilliant idea 16).
- There are some really fascinating and unusual books on your reading list (brilliant idea 48, and the resources section at the end).
- Brand is now about you (brilliant idea 35).

And you'll be reminded that:
- Leadership starts with you (brilliant idea 5).
- It's generally about profit (brilliant idea 9).
- Management models do make the world go round (brilliant idea 12).
- Good is no longer good enough (brilliant idea 19).
- You need a personal development plan (brilliant idea 28).

How might you use it?
- Read one idea/week and implement the idea in your business.
- As part of a group project for business improvement at work.
- Read it alongside your full or part-time MBA in order to ensure that you can see the wood for the trees.
- To decide whether you do want to commit the time to an MBA, proper.

And me? Well, I am very fortunate in that I work in both the mainstream commercial world and the academic environment. I consult and I teach; I research and I practise. I am therefore confident that what I'm offering you here is what you really need, the very best of what you really need.

There is no doubt about it, the business world just gets tougher and tougher. But there's equally no doubt that those who invest in thinking differently, in pulling ahead from the crowd, in constantly seeking fresh brilliant ideas are not just those who survive, but also those who thrive.

Let's start.

You'll notice the symbol at the start of a few of the ideas in this book. These chapters have a bit more information such as further reading and website links, which you can find starting on page 229.

1. Start thinking again!

You know that you have become stale; that's why the MBA is attractive to you. Let's get those synaptic pathways sparking again.

How to think creatively, how to think critically, reflectively and laterally. How to think — full stop.

Probably your greatest asset is your thinking ability. Consequently, one of the easiest and fastest things you can do to improve your attractiveness to your current employer and/or to future employers is to develop this asset. Equally, if you are running your own business, how would it be if you could think laterally about discount challenges or find time to think reflectively about your team? Exactly.

Thinking brings out the best in your inherent or genetic intelligence. Thinking enables you to reveal more of your emotional intelligence. Thinking allows growth, problem solving and fun. Thinking allows you to feel fully alive. So what goes wrong? Well, we all get so busy that we stop thinking and act on autocue; we've been here before so we'll do what worked then; we get dulled, we feel trapped. Let's break all of that. Think!

Here is some 'what and how' on thinking.

Here's an idea for you...

Take a walk, about thirty minutes would be ideal. Leave your phone behind. Don't take any reading matter or anyone to chat to. Just take a walk on your own. Finally, as you head off on your walk, don't set off with any agenda in mind, anything you are trying to solve, a problem you wish to work on: just walk. If you are like many high performers, you'll go through these stages: firstly irritation at the process (that, by the way, is stress release), then noticing things more (that's your senses working again) and finally insight (and that's your brain working again).

Firstly, do more thinking. That means taking the time to do it by perhaps, surprisingly, doing more 'nothing'. Work, especially in the business world, is now so busy and there's so much communication for you to receive that it is increasingly difficult to communicate with yourself. So take a break – not a cigarette, coffee or chat break – but just take a break and do nothing. This is known as reflective thinking and allows you to demonstrate your reflective intelligence; the ability to be smart because you have given something consideration. You have considered the pricing policy; you have considered what you will say at the kick-off, and that consideration has added considerable value. The fantastic thing about reflective thinking is that you don't need to do anything; if you do, you are not reflecting! You do not need to work or strain at it, either; if you do, you are not reflecting. It's easy: just 'allow' it. This is the kind of thinking which often happens in the shower. You know it works, so encourage it.

Then there is creative thinking or lateral thinking (the latter is specifically the author Edward De Bono's term). This is looking at things in a 'non-linear' way. For example, if you are trying to improve cash flow, it is tempting to reduce costs and, of course, there is often a bit of slack so that is no bad thing. But what about if you increased prices at the same time, or sacked some unprofitable clients? Thinking laterally or creatively is sometimes known as thinking 'outside the box'. To be good at it, you do need to know what is in the box, that is the facts and the current situation. Creative thinking is not an excuse for a lack of discipline, and one serious competitive differentiator you can develop is the ability to get creative thinking happening in your organisation while at the same time being great at implementing or making things happen.

And critical thinking? That's essential, and very powerful when coupled with the previous two. This is questioning, probing. Often, well-established statements such as 'that's not the way we do things around here' are taken for granted. Critical thinking examines them: well, what would happen if we did do it differently? 'Our customers want more support'. OK. In what ways? And always? Critical thinking particularly respects the fact that one definition of intelligence is the ability to hold two different ideas in your head at the same time. Critical thinkers avoid the common temptation to generalise ('we must get big to make money') or polarise ('there's no way they'll look at us until we have an office in the US.').

Don't be trapped by the dogma of other people's thinking. Steve Jobs

How did it go?

Q. Can anyone become more creative?

A. Yes, definitely. Remember that your competence at anything is a mixture of nature (your genes, of course) and nurture (the way you 'developed' or were brought up). The essential idea here is to do the maximum you can to nurture your nature; to develop yourself to be the best version of you that you can. How? Well, the three Ms: Mindset, Mechanics and Momentum. Mindset is simple: 'I can become more creative'. Mechanics? There are plenty of tips and tricks to develop creativity. Here are two – reversing the current situation (for instance, 'instead of outsourcing, let's think for a moment what would happen if we actually bought our own warehouse') and brainstorming. Here free association is encouraged in a non-critical environment in the belief that amongst the ridiculous ideas some gems will appear. Finally, there's momentum – continuing to give yourself opportunities to be creative.

Q. To be honest I hate sitting around thinking, and people do consider me a real man of action. I'd much rather get on with things. Is that wrong, then?

A. Hey, action is vital! You can be creative, critical and reflective but if you don't do anything with it, then all the work has been wasted. But, equally, action without a little reflection or lateral and/or critical thinking can be a waste of good energy and intention. As always – balance is the key.

2. Know your thought leader 1: Michael Porter

Michael Porter: man of strategy, man of the 'value-chain'. Is this any use in the real world? And how can you get the essence of his thick books in a few minutes?

Don't worry, I'll give it to you! And more importantly I'll show you how you can use it in your own business or advise your clients on what is important...

Who is Michael Porter? He's a professor at Harvard Business School whose main 'thing' is strategy, on which he has written significant books and articles. Importantly, though, he's not just a writer and spends a large part of his time on the lecture circuit and advising large organisations. His most famous and probably most widely read book is *Competitive Strategy*. He is most definitely a key thought leader that you need to consider as you get to grips with your instant MBA, and I can summarise Porter's two key ideas for you.

Idea 1: five forces analysis
The five forces framework is invaluable as a starting point for determining an organisation's (either yours or your client's) competitive position in the marketplace. It won't produce a number for you but it will give you a good qualitative feeling.

The five forces are:

1. The threat of substitute products, e.g. downloading films from the Internet versus buying them from a video store.
2. The threat of current competitors, e.g. the overstocked sandwich market in the UK.
3. The threat of new players with a totally fresh approach, e.g. the new luxury chocolate market.
4. The bargaining power of suppliers, e.g. negotiating with a top brand name.
5. The bargaining power of customers, e.g. customers using Internet shopping sites which compare prices.

Here's a practical example, looking at each of the five forces above, for a local café that has three branches in a seaside city:

1. Substitute products – coffee 'to go' from American brands
2. Current competitors – existing cafés extending their opening hours
3. New players – some of the hotels opening café bars
4. Bargaining power of suppliers – the high price of real Italian espresso machines
5. Bargaining power of customers – people switching to buying on price for their coffee 'to go'.

Idea 2: the value chain

A value chain is a chain of events. Products progress through events in the chain in order, and at each event the product gains some value. For instance, a financial planning software package may be supplied with hotline support; this is clearly value which has been added to the basic software product. Value chain analysis is particularly useful in that it helps you focus your thinking on what adds cost, and hence appropriately reducing it, and on what creates differentiation – and increasing that. Now for the practical example. That software company actually includes 180 days of free 24–7 technical support for its new product. The free support could be a major differentiator over its competitor but clearly comes at a cost. Value chain analysis encourages the producers of the software to become very clear on the relative values of these two items.

Using Porter's ideas

Set up an off site meeting lasting at least four hours; ensure there are no interruptions at all. Explain the concepts of five forces analysis and the value chain to your team. Split them into small teams of about three, then ask them to use those concepts to come back with ideas on how the competitiveness of the organisation might be improved. Ask for the ideas to be presented succinctly and then debate them briefly with strict time controls in place. Finally decide some actions, even if your action is no action, and assign a project manager to each. If you want to use Porter's ideas with clients, just apply the same process – you are the facilitator of the sessions, of course. Ensure a time line is established and an ongoing project is created. They'll need to set up some measures of success, too.

Here's an idea for you...

Which are you going to work on? Your own business or that of a client of yours? You choose. Now take a sheet of paper or, if one happens to be handy, a whiteboard – that would be perfect. Think about your product and write down every stage it goes through before getting to the customer. There might be two or twenty or even more stages, but write them all down. Now think about what extra things – value – are added at each stage. Once you've given that some consideration, could anything be done to add more?

There is no best. Competing on the same dimensions just makes it hard for customers to choose. Instead, you have to compete to be unique. The essence of strategy is finding out what your unique advantage is.

Michael Porter

7

How did it go?

Q. Is Porter correct in his five forces and value chain methodologies?

A. The answer I'm about to give is true of any thought leader's work: yes and no! Porter clearly uses examples which defend his points and, generally, does so elegantly. His critics can find plenty of examples where his theories don't work (or apparently not, anyway). But that's not really the point – the point is that large numbers of those practising management theory and, perhaps more importantly, those leading and running organisations find that Porter gives them a structure for their thinking in the tricky area of what makes them competitive, and what sustains that competitiveness. If Porter had found a definite, 100% guaranteed principle that always worked – well, that would be truly remarkable. If you are trying to improve your business or a client's business, then his work is a great place to start.

Q. We are a ten-person building firm. How do I use these ideas?

A. Book two days of planning separated by two weeks. Don't cancel those days. On the first do the five forces analysis and on the second analyse your value chain and make it better as a result of your five forces analysis. Take action and there'll be no stopping you!

3. What's the experience?

It's not about service – it's about the experience. Disney got it. Starbucks gets it and, increasingly, so does M&S. Do you get it and, more importantly, can you create it?

A wow experience, that is. Something which causes your customers to feel a positive tingle, to come back and back and back. And you just take more money to the bank.

It's a tough old global market out there: the competition gets tougher and tougher. Customers get choosier and choosier. And product differentiation is harder to maintain. But, wait: at the 'hard' product level that is certainly true, a latte is still a latte. A small hatchback is just a small hatchback, a bank is a bank. OK, you can add an extra shot to your latte or free SatNav to your hatchback or new, faster ATMs to your bank, but how long can that differentiation be maintained? You're right, not long. Do remember, though, that differentiation is about three factors – company or brand, products and people. And it's the people which can create the real difference, who can create a wow experience. You see, everyone knows that's no longer about the commodity. It's no longer just about the brand. It really is about service, of course. But it's actually about more than that: it's about experience.

Here's an idea for you...

Write a story, write a scenario about your company or product. Take a few of the basic ingredients, tell a story and see where it goes. The most important thing is to write. Don't plan or prepare. Don't, at this stage, worry about syntax or grammar; simply write. If you do this you'll be amazed at the ideas which are revealed from your deeper consciousness. Wondering how to tackle it? Think about Levi Jeans – what would you do with them? After all, what a story – cowboys, men who were men, great girls in great trousers. How could you create differentiated experience from that?

You know the Disney story. A man has a dream, a dream to create a perfect theme park – one which is safe for children and a delight for their parents, a place where there would be no litter and all the staff would be courteous. True, the rides are fantastic, but what's really different is the people. (Remember how there were initial problems in Euro Disney as the staff didn't get the idea?)

What about Starbucks? Is it about coffee? Sort of. It's great coffee, of course, and their lovely, well-designed shops. But the staff and the music and the aroma all pull together to create Howard Schulz's 'third place' experience. Not home, not work, but a place where you can go to chill.

There are plenty of other examples. How about Innocent Juices? Is that really all about fresh fruit juice? No. It's about the friendly 'banter' of their bottles, about their quirky website, about things like the banana phone. It's a total experience, and so is the new M&S too, with their amazing advertisements for food. The stores are now a whole lot fresher, and the whole thing is a much better 'experience'. Of course.

Here's the bottom line. To pull ahead in what's known as the New World of Work, you must give your customers a powerful and positive and enlivening experience, one which is so good that they want to return. And how? Here are a few 'experience enliveners' you might consider for your organisation:

- Simplicity: less is more. In a busy world people appreciate it if things are really simple (forms to fill in, websites to navigate, airports to reach), elegant (where exactly are the English wines in this mess of a shop?) and straightforward (how do I complain?). This might be as basic as signage in a supermarket which helps people find the cereals or as sophisticated as your website. But less is generally more.
- People: great people make such a good experience. How about helpful people on the end of a phone compared to robotic call centres? How about having enough baristas in your coffee shop? How about people so helpful that customers want to return? Yes, they are only buying a light bulb at the moment, but give them a great experience and they will come to you for their next dishwasher.
- Easy: stress-less. Here's a good example. There are plenty of trolleys at the airport and they're free, too. It's obvious where you need to queue, the signage is brilliant and clear, and the whole place has been planned to minimise walking.
- Design: great design. This creates an even better user experience – whether that's proper labelling and careful choice of colours or reduced wrapping and packaging and being more ecologically sound. Keep instructions helpful and provide simple start-up guides, as well as clear advice about where to go if it all goes wrong.
- Worthwhile: having purpose. Increasing numbers of people want to help the planet rather than damage it. How green are you? How fair trade are you?
- Lead, not just serve. Provide what people want, sure, but take it further and anticipate their needs.

Our brains deal exclusively with special-case experiences.

Buckminster Fuller, *Operating Manual for Spaceship Earth, 1963*

How did it go?

Q. Can't experiences simply be replicated?

A. Yes; theoretically Starbucks, Apple or Disney could all be copied. But in reality they are not and that is because an essential part of the experience is soft skills, and soft skills are hard to measure, hard to replicate. And few people – unlike you – really get that. Yes, you can literally copy technology (leaving aside copyright issues) but you can only 'model' soft skills; to do that requires constant attention and energy and only a few players are up to it. But one of them could be you.

Q. Won't a 'wow' experience eventually lose its shine?

A. Yes; it's happening to Disney and Starbucks has been called 'the next McDonald's'. But that's where great marketing and great MBA thinking comes in: stay ahead of the crowd. What's the new experience you can offer? How can you be even better? There's always a way.

4. Presenting ideas is not about PowerPoint

You'll live or die by your ability to present. And you'll die a slow death – or maybe your audience will – if you keep doing that old PowerPoint slide stuff.

Here's how to present 'unplugged', how to present with passion — and how to get your audience to buy your ideas.

Business is about ideas. The better the ideas the more exciting it is, as those better ideas will make more money, save money, open up a new market opportunity or… well, the list is endless. But an idea loses its power unless it can be communicated, rapidly communicated, and to the relevant number of people. Guess what? The presentation is born.

In the Old World of Work, the presentation mainly revolved around you, the person, the individual. Visual aids, as they were then known, were simple (flipcharts, for instance), time-consuming to produce (professional overhead projector slides) or expensive (35 mm slides). Although those latter challenges were a little frustrating, it kept a natural limitation to the amount of distraction away from the main presenter that could be managed. Then twenty years ago, riding on the back of the personal computing revolution, PowerPoint arrived.

PowerPoint – now a Microsoft product – made it easy to give a 'professional appearance' to your slides and also to generate high numbers of them. Rapidly,

13

Here's an idea for you...

Take a slide deck you regularly use; something lengthy such as forty-five minutes would be ideal. How many slides have you got? Really? That's frightening. OK, decide that the next time you give this presentation you will use only half that number. Go through the deck and remove any bad slides. Then introduce both a story and an activity. Next time your audience will love it – and so will you.

the art of real presenting was lost. So what exactly are the problems that you should avoid?

Don't use PowerPoint badly

There is nothing inherently 'bad' about PowerPoint. To suggest that would be as if I was to blame Excel for a poor cash flow. No, it's the poor use of PowerPoint which is the problem. Here are the top poor uses:

- Script on a slide. It is very easy to write your presentation directly on to PowerPoint; consequently many people end up just presenting a script. Write your presentation first and then decide if and how many slides you need.
- Busy, busy, busy. Busy does not equate to extra value; it simply causes confusion. Put less on your slides, fewer words and fewer bullets, because less is definitely more. Be very careful about embedded videos and/or too many effects. Don't do something just because you can; it doesn't necessarily help the audience.
- Brand power. Not every slide needs to have your logo on it or be in corporate colours. Too much of this 'brand power' is a distraction.

Do use PowerPoint well

Go back to the original term: visual aids. A slide was meant to help the concept and not hinder it. Hence a PowerPoint slide is good for:

- Graphs. Brilliant stories, brilliant body language cannot replace a simple line graph if you are trying to explain growth in product sales. Graphs and pie charts can be great for explaining points, but keep it simple. If you must have three lines on one graph, perhaps consider building the graph one line at a time to help understanding.

- Pictures. For example, you could show what a new product will look like – but show it at the right time, though. If the picture is ahead of your explanation people will be looking at it, not listening to you. Introduce the product, talk a bit; show the picture; pause. Then carry on.
- Schematic: 'This is our account management structure'. Show the structure of the department and allow people to take it in by stopping talking, and then – perhaps – take questions.
- Quotation: Something like '"Make a dent in the universe", Steve Jobs'. And don't read the quote to your audience: they can do that.
- Drama. Your slide shows a single number: 42. This intrigues people and they wonder what it's about; you can then explain.

Present 'unplugged' more often. Work on your:
- State. Your state will create their state. Be enthusiastic and your audience will become so; be boring and they will become bored.
- Space. Don't stand behind a lectern; get out into the audience and connect with them.
- Story. Tell stories; people love it and remember them.
- Structure. Get a logical flow which people can follow – a start, a middle and an end!
- Spikes. Create change (a spike) to re-engage the drifting and wandering mind. A question, an activity, a story…
- Storyboard. You are a film director: plan your start, your ending, even your car chase.
- Slides. Then, and only then, decide what slides you need. You'll find you won't need many, which is the way it should be.

Power corrupts and PowerPoint corrupts absolutely. Vint Cerf, Internet pioneer

15

How did it go?

Q. Don't you think there are huge expectations that a 'professional' will automatically use PowerPoint?

A. Yes, but as a top MBA student you know that to be amazing you need to sometimes step around people's expectations, wouldn't you agree? What people really expect is a decent presentation which, unfortunately, they think means PowerPoint. If you can do it another better way, they will be delighted. Really delighted. And they will remember you and your message.

Q. I find having lots of PowerPoint slides with all my words on gives me confidence. What do I do about my nerves?

A. Well, they *will* give you confidence – what you are doing, of course, is essentially reading your script to the audience. To be honest, you hardly need to be there. You are adding very little value. Here's a suggestion. Be willing to endure a little pain now and learn how to present without your 100% PowerPoint dependence. It will repay the effort many times over in terms of future career opportunities.

5. Are you a leader?

Let's forget the endless navel-gazing discussions about leadership. Let's get on with it. Let's live by the consequences of our actions. Let's make it happen. That's real leadership!

If there is one skill which cannot be, dare I say will never be, automated, it's the skill of leadership. If you don't have this skill, you're vulnerable.

As you begin to work through, study and master your personal MBA, one thing will strike you: there are a few topics which come up time and time again in different formats and aspects, like project management or certain elements of finance and accounting, for example. There is one, however, which tops the list all of the time; it's on the critical path: leadership. Nothing happens without effective leadership, so what do you need to know about this subject?

Firstly, you need to be confident in the knowledge that anyone can become a leader. Of course, history has shown time and time again that in any field – be it politics or medicine or music or whatever – there are certain 'naturals' who will rise to the top, whatever might happen. So certainly there is a genetic, or 'nature', element to leadership. But that doesn't stop any of us 'nurturing our nature' or becoming better at leadership. Secondly there are a huge number of models

Here's an idea for you...

Write down the names of some great leaders you are aware of in any field – past or present, famous or not, real or fictional. They could come from sport, politics, the military, industry, teaching… Try and get ten names. They might be brand names (such as Richard Branson), they might be just personal to you. I expect you'll have a very varied list. Your mum, Winston Churchill, your old history teacher, Gandhi… now, what do they all have in common? Try and capture it in just three words. What are the three words? Compare your answers with mine opposite.

about leadership out there. All have their quirky variants, their own proponents, but there are some factors which are generally agreed upon. Let's look at them, as they can help you become an outstanding leader.

Mindset: leadership starts with you, part 1

In the New World of Work, leadership is increasingly a mindset rather than a job title. It is something to be taken rather than waited for. It is an approach rather than a job specification. Here's an example. Alf, Vip and Jane are all graduate trainees in a start-up software company. Alf and Vip spend a lot of their day complaining that the training they were promised at their interviews isn't happening. Jane has been out and bought some books, charged them to her expenses, spends part of each day studying – and she will do that until someone stops her. She realises that leadership is not about waiting for permission; it's about getting on with it. You can always apologise later.

Lead yourself: leadership starts with you, part 2

To be a great leader you must be able to lead yourself. Can you? For example, can you:

- Get your report in on time?
- Get up early?
- Go through a whole day without blaming anyone else?
- Be accountable for your actions?

- Plan? And review?
- Manage your time?
- Invest in relationships?

You can? Excellent; you have the basis of outstanding leadership.

Leadership is situational

So leadership starts with mindset. It continues as you develop the ability to lead yourself. Then, as you move your focus to the leadership of others, you must realise that it is situational. Ken Blanchard was probably the first to fully articulate this point, that essentially the leadership of others depends on responding appropriately to the combination of their current competence and their current motivation. For example, if someone is highly motivated and highly competent you can simply leave them to it after the correct briefing; this is known as delegation. If someone is new to the job or role and thus not very competent, yet, but is also highly motivated, then they simply need direction. Good leaders recognise that their default style is not perfect for all situations and constantly adjust it as the occasion demands.

Answer

Here's my answer to the exercise about three words which describe your personal selection of leaders. I have done this exercise with thousands of people over the years, from schoolchildren to senior businessmen, and in places from London to Singapore. People always agree on three concepts and they often use the same three words as well: vision, energy and communication. Great leaders must be able to articulate the journey and give hope that the journey can be accomplished – that's vision. They must be able to energise people, to raise their standards, and they must also be able to communicate how the vision will be achieved.

We must be the change we wish to see in the world. Gandhi

19

How did it go?

Q. Surely I need to be promoted to manager or team leader before I can really lead anyone?

A. No – and this is a point which, once you 'get', you will never forget! Leadership is just something you can do. During a day at home or at work you will be given endless situations which give you the opportunity to lead, inspire, guide, give people direction or give them hope. Or not. If you do the former you are leading.

Q. So, is there a difference between management and leadership?

A. Now, there's a big topic! To a certain extent this is the stuff of never-ending debate much of which, if I'm honest, is irrelevant to the day-to-day practice of management and leadership. But having said that, most would agree that management tends to be more about perspiration where leadership is about inspiration, about a definite job title as opposed to leadership's choice, about tactics rather than strategy, and about mechanics rather than methodology.

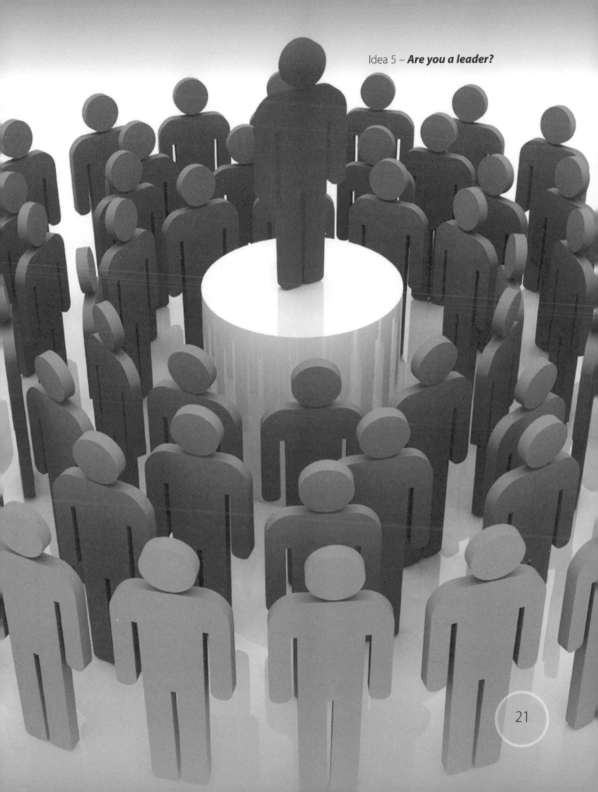

6. It's not about time: it's about decisions

You will never, ever have enough time. That's because you are an interesting and interested person and you live in interesting times.

If you are out of time, you need to get better at making the right choices. Forget time management; get great at choice management instead.

Have you ever said 'I don't have enough time' or 'If only there were more hours in the day'? Have you ever heard any of your clients say 'It's just a lack of time' or 'Well, there's not enough time to consider that'?

What about your business colleagues? Have you come across them saying 'This is really urgent', 'We simply don't have time for that planning, we've got a year-end to close here' or 'That's not important at the moment'?

Of course you have. If there is one topic you can guarantee will occur in any business conversation anywhere in the world, it's the topic of time. Phrases like '100% of the time', complaints about the lack of it, urgency, important… It's *the* business issue and in this busy, busy world it's becoming more of one. Here's the fundamental problem: it doesn't matter how brilliant you are, what fantastic ideas you have, who is sponsoring you – if you don't have time to implement change, if you don't have time to run an off-site meeting, if you don't have time to respond to customers, then your business will die.

In the Old World of Work, in the original MBA courses, a topic such as 'time management' could be dealt with in a one-liner. It was usually something along the lines of: '…decide what needs to be done, put them in priority order and work through them'. Open any management or leadership MBA textbook from the 1950s, 60s, or even the 70s or 80s, and that's the suggestion you would have received and it would have worked. Time and decision management was able to rely on:

- A stable and static environment. Whether you were in cars or clothes, music or consultancy, little changed in your world from year to year, even decade to decade. Customers were predictable; competitors were reliable and understood. There was absolutely no need to rush around and a long lunch would do nicely.
- A larger workforce. Remember that word delegation? Laughable now, isn't it? To whom, exactly, do you delegate these days? It's rare to find any real support beyond your laptop.
- Fewer interruptions. Phone calls, of course, but only on a land line; mail, of course, but once a day in the post and occasionally dropping into your in tray.
- Slower interruptions. Factors such as typing, post and distance all ensured that you were the fastest thing around.

Of course in the New World of Work, things are very different:
- There's much more uncertainty: 'Which market are we in? Coffee? Experiences? Music?'

> ### Here's an idea for you...
>
> Take a sheet of paper. Put the word IMPORTANT across the top. Don't write anything on this paper unless it really is important. Now draw a line down the middle, vertically. Head the left-hand side with URGENT and the right-hand side with NON-URGENT. Fill both sides with the things that you have to do and put them in the appropriate place. Did you rush to put things on 'urgent' and find it difficult to identify stuff for the other side? Perhaps the non-urgent things are actually vital (career, health…)? Cross out 'non-urgent' and put 'investing'.

- The workforce is reduced and expensive, or on the other side of the globe.
- Constant interruptions, with email being the killer.
- Rapid interruptions. No longer is there any escape; it is harder and harder to find time to think.

So, now that you have reminded yourself of the scale of the problem, what is to be done? Here are some practical suggestions:

- Accept that you will never have enough time. Stop trying to create more time: all you do is steal it from your golf, theatre going or life in general.
- Decide to do a little less, and do what you do decide to execute so well that it has an impact. That's instead of doing lots of things which count for little.
- Decide to ensure that what you do is of value and will count in the long term.
- Prioritise against pay-off, not against what's easy or who is shouting the loudest.
- Be aware that often what seems 'not urgent' now (e.g. planning, team building, long-term strategy) turns out to be vital in the longer term. So do some non-urgent things or, more correctly, 'investing' things now.
- Push back on interruptions so that your greatest asset, your brain, can work again.
- Choose, don't react.

Overall, don't manage time; manage your decisions. Slow down to the speed of your thinking as it's your greatest asset, and do a little less to achieve a whole lot more.

I love deadlines. I like the whooshing sound they make as they go by. Douglas Adams

How did it go?

Q. Doesn't this kind of thinking stifle creativity?

A. Absolutely not. Let's be clear: being focused, making the right decision, investing for the future all helps your future creativity. Or, to put it more directly, you cannot think outside the box unless you know what the box is. Great time or decision management is about identifying the box exactly.

Q. But I do have to do everything… How can I do this too?

A. Right, you don't have to do it all; I want to be firm on this one. It is more of a mindset issue than a practical issue. You have to realise that nobody can do everything and if you do attempt to do so, then you will start doing things badly and end up burning out. So you need to make a decision on this topic and make it now.

7. Get big, get special or get out

Don't mess about. In the New World of Work there are a few simple strategies for making money. You don't need to read any Harvard Business Reviews to be clear on this.

They are well established: get big, get special or forget it. Here's how to choose the right approach and how to develop it.

Look around you. Who makes money in business? Write it down: Microsoft, Starbucks, Fox, Google, perhaps the *Guardian* newspapers in the UK? Now ask yourself how these organisations make money. The answer, in its simplest form, is that they are either big, like Microsoft or Google, or they are special, like Fox, Guardian newspapers or Innocent Juices. Of course some businesses try to be both – Starbucks leaps to mind – but you will notice that as Starbucks has become bigger, it has also become less special. Maybe Starbucks can make the transition and keep making money; maybe it needs to accept that it can make more money from a different kind of (volume) customer. But everyone would agree that Starbucks began by being special.

What does being big mean?

It means that you gain benefits that come from…

■ sheer size, such as having several branches in an area so that if staff are sick you can move some in from another branch;

■ market share, so that you can negotiate harder with your suppliers as they want to get their product to consumers via your channel;

■ low marketing costs as 'everybody knows about you'.

You get big by customers loving what you do. Consequently you grow organically (which, interestingly, is back to the 'get special' strategy). You can also get big by having sufficient money so that you can acquire other organisations. Microsoft, for example, is less special than it once was, but it has a significant war chest from those days which it can use. Being big makes you money because your organisation is able to keep costs down and, as you grow, is able to reduce costs even more. This in turn maintains and/or grows margin and consequently increases profitability.

Here's an idea for you...

Take a client of yours and answer the following questions, rapidly and in writing. What business is your client in? Who are their customers? Who are their competitors? How big are they compared to their competitors? How different are they? On a scale of one to ten, where would you place their overall competitive strategy (where ten is brilliant and one is highly vulnerable)? If it's not ten, what needs to be done, when, and who can make it happen? Look back at what you have written – do you have a plan with some distinct action? How long did it take you – ten to fifteen minutes? That's serious MBA thinking.

27

What does being special mean?

It means that there are one or more aspects of your business which are unique to you, such as…

- extra useful features on your product;
- brilliant customer service.

You get special, initially, often through a bright idea, which you then implement. Generally, though, it's through the old cliché: 99% perspiration and 1% inspiration. Being special makes you money because you can charge more if you are special and, assuming that what is special is also desirable, customers cannot choose the competition in preference to you; you're unique or almost so. Both of these factors lead to better margin and better profitability.

If there is nothing very special about your work, no matter how hard you apply yourself you won't get noticed, and that increasingly means you won't get paid much either.

Michael Goldhaber, in Wired

How did it go?

Q. *There are just two options: special or big. Isn't this a gross simplification?*

A. In one sense, yes. When ideas are simple everyone can normally understand them and then begin to apply them, which is what this is all about: immediate help and assistance. Does it cover all of the nuances that are involved in a business making money? Of course not, but it's a great place to start. Many entrepreneurs try to make a profitable business simply by copying a business that is doing well. By definition a copy is not special and in the early days it will not be big. It's likely, therefore, to be at best a struggle to make money, or at worst a failure. This may be a simple idea, but that certainly does not make it less valid.

Q. *I have done an analysis of my own business and I'm not special, I'm not big. Am I doomed?*

A. No. Definitely not. Firstly, well done on doing the analysis: it may not give you much consolation, but you have become a little special simply by doing it. Very few organisations do sufficient thinking and strategy around their business and in particular on what makes their business successful and what might make it more successful. Whether you are a small one-man-band consultancy or a large manufacturer, that's the first stage: to do an audit and see how things stand at the moment. So now you know, and they don't look too good. What are you going to do, how can you create difference, where can you start getting benefits of scale? You need to take a little time out with your team (if you have one) and do some thinking and brainstorming. Simply keep answering these two questions: 'How can we get more special?' and 'How can we get large enough to benefit from economies of scale?' Once you have a great list of ideas, ask this: 'How can we make these things happen?'

8. Know your thought leader 2: Gary Hamel

He of Leading the Revolution *fame and – unfortunately for him – the one who used Enron as his 'model' case study.*

Still, everyone makes mistakes and you can still learn a lot from Hamel's ideas.

Gary Hamel is a visiting professor of Strategic Management at London Business School. His key theory is the concept of core competencies, and he has written some significant books and articles about this as well as other matters. Importantly, though, he is not just a writer and spends a large part of his time on the lecture circuit and advising large organisations, the latter via his management consulting firm, Strategos. His most famous and probably most widely read book is *Leading the Revolution* and his most recent work is *The Future of Management*. He is most definitely a thought leader to include in your MBA studies. Hamel's key ideas can be summarised as follows…

Idea 1: core competency
The concept of core competency is Gary Hamel's first and most formalised management idea; it was published with C. K. Prahalad in *Competing for the Future* in 1990. A core competency is something that a company does well. According to Hamel and Prahalad it should meet three conditions. It must:

- Provide benefits to the customer.
- Be difficult for competitors to copy.
- Be transferable to other situations, e.g. other markets or products.

Here's an example from retailing. The supermarket group Tesco has been an early adopter of the concept of profiling and understanding customer buying habits; a good example of this was the early development of the Tesco loyalty card. This core competency – profiling and understanding buying habits – has been used to its advantage in creating its successful online shopping business. On the other hand M&S, despite for some time refusing any credit cards apart from its own in order to build its own database, never really embraced the online world or developed profiling as a core competence. Its core competence is its food business, Simply Foods, however.

Here's an idea for you...

Think about your organisation – or that of one of your clients – and ask yourself whether things would be done differently if it was being launched today. It doesn't matter how old the business is; do this even if it has been established for only a couple of months – there's always something you'd like to change. Be creative in your thinking and try to be objective as well. Use a large piece of paper (or a whiteboard) and write down all the things you would prefer to have been done differently, and why. How could they be made to happen now?

Idea 2: reinvention and revolution

Hamel has stressed the need for reinvention in *Leading the Revolution* and *The Future of Management*. The essential idea from these books is that business has changed and must become revolutionary to survive. From *Leading the Revolution* comes part 1: facing up to the revolution, which stresses that change is now a daily occurrence. Part 2 is funding the revolution – innovate or die – and part 3, ignite the revolution, emphasises that you must be an activist in order to make the revolution happen. Part 4, sustaining the revolution, gives ten key rules for sustaining a business. The essential idea from *The Future of Management* is that organisations are working with an outdated business model which does not allow them to move quickly; in the current business environment this model just has to change.

Using Hamel's ideas

The best way to begin applying some of Hamel's concepts is to set up an off-site session for your team. Expect it to last at least half a day, and make sure you're not going to be interrupted. Explain core competencies and the need for reinvention and revolution, and divide people into small mini-teams (keep the groups to a maximum of three members). Then ask them to use those concepts to come back with snappy ideas on how the organisation's competitiveness could be improved. When they return, discuss the results – with strict time controls – and decide on some actions. Make sure all the actions you decide to undertake are allocated to specific project managers. If you're consulting, you can initiate the same process with your clients.

Our starting proposition is that competition between firms is as much a race for competence mastery as it is for market position and market power. Gary Hamel

How did it go?

Q. Is Hamel right when he suggests that a business must become revolutionary to change?

A. Well, yes and no! Naturally Hamel uses examples which defend his points, but you would expect that. There are plenty of other examples which his critics can use to demonstrate that his theories don't work, but that doesn't mean they're not valid. His reputation suffered significantly because his main example in *Leading the Revolution* was Enron, possibly the worst (with hindsight, of course) that any researcher could have chosen. Perhaps with more thorough research it might have been discovered that Enron did not follow Hamel's theories or – as is often an accusation levelled at management theorists – that the study was just too artificial and/or superficial. However, Hamel's ideas have given very many people – including those leading large global organisations – a useful way of thinking about competitiveness and change. Importantly, unlike Michael Porter but similarly to Tom Peters, two other significant thought leaders, he is particularly good at giving you the inspiration to start.

Q. I'm a one-man band, but I love Hamel's ideas. Where should I begin?

A. Definitely go for core competency. If you can get that aspect right – and you can – you will be doing better than many organisations thousands of times larger than you.

9. Anybody can make money: can you make profit?

There are various forms of money. And the danger with business schools is that it can all get too theoretical…

I'm going to ensure your understanding of this topic is so good that you are standing up and shouting for profit!

Here's how to make money. I thought you would like the sound of that!

What is profit?

In its simplest terms, it's the money from sales of the organisation less the costs of the organisation. Importantly it is distinguished from revenue, which is simply the money from the sales which the organisation makes. It is also distinguished from cash flow, which is the coming in and going out of cash. An organisation can fail, even when ultimately it should be profitable, because it has not managed its flow of cash and runs out of it. And, clearly, revenue alone is not an indicator of a viable business.

Profit is important to an organisation because, firstly, it is a clear, visible and ultimately published measure of how well a business is doing. For good or bad, people will measure your success to a certain extent by looking at your profitability. Secondly, it is a reward to those who run the business. They have taken risks with their time and money and resources. If there is no reward, what is the incentive to continue taking those risks? Thirdly, profits provide funds for expansion in the future and, finally, a business that does not make money will ultimately fail.

How to make profit…

Here are six straightforward – but often neglected – ways for your business or those of your clients to make profit.

- Pricing. Profit will originate from the money made on products (hard) or services (soft). The money made, of course, is arithmetically calculated by price less cost. To a certain extent there may well not be a lot you can do about costs, but you can often be more imaginative about prices. Do not be frightened to increase your prices, for example. If there is a lot of customer resistance you can always lower them later. Consider having some premium price products. By all means give discount for volume but ensure your accountant has done the calculations; it can take a surprisingly large increase in volume to make up for even small discounts.

- Manage costs. Do whatever you can to keep costs down by choosing your suppliers well, managing your infrastructure, measuring costs and encouraging your employees to keep costs down. Ensure expenses policies are

Here's an idea for you…

Talk to three groups of people either on the phone or by email. The three groups are your customer or your client's customer, your client (or ask yourself) and your bank manager or those in the world of finance – for instance, your accountant. Ask them this simple question: what makes for a successful business in their view? Summarise the results in fifty words or less. You'll notice a dilemma. Customers want great product at low cost, business people have a dream or vision to execute, the financial person wants growth, excellent shareholder return and profit. You have to balance those three demands.

documented and adhered to. If there is a loophole which allows someone to fly business class, then they will. Don't begrudge them the extra comfort if it is appropriate, but that's a heck of a cost compared to economy.

- Measures. Ensure profitability is measured, especially to the level of detail which allows you to identify something like a product which is very profitable or is not price sensitive, or a product line which is not profitable and should be removed. Identify which customers or markets or countries are profitable for you. Understand the reasons behind those results, too, as that may well allow you to create more products with extra profitability.
- Manage cash. Without cash it doesn't matter how profitable you are. You need cash to work the business on a day-to-day basis.
- Training and development. Teach everybody to realise the importance of revenue, profit and cash flow, and to understand the essential differences between them. In particular remove the naivety that some employees can have that 'revenue is all'. Run a negotiation course and teach them how to sell value and not be defensive about prices.
- Devolve responsibility. Give responsibility for profitability to all concerned. It is a common mistake to reward sales people simply by the revenue they've generated, for example. That may well encourage too much deal making, discounting and consequent low profitability.

The promise of every product and service is a better life. Profits are the prize for delivering on the promise.

Patrick Dixon, *Building a Better Business.*

How did it go?

Q. Is profit the only measure of a business's success?

A. Absolutely not. A business's health – especially that of larger organisations – can be measured in many different ways and also specifically by a range of ratios, such as a liquidity ratio that measures the availability of cash to pay debt. A summary of such ratios, when understood, can give an excellent overview of an organisation's short- and long-term viability. Having said all that, profit understanding is an excellent place to start when working on your own business or when consulting to improve one of your client's businesses.

Q. Is profit always good?

A. Basically, yes. Without profit, it is difficult to grow. But profit is generally taxed and so it might be wise to plan your profit to ensure that you make the profit which you need, but no more. That's where a good accountant should be helping you. In a very small business it may be that the sole purpose is enjoyment and that the business serves its purpose as long as it breaks even.

10. Thank goodness: no case studies and no syndicate work!

Business schools are a lot of fun: a year of fresh ideas, new friends and new thinking. But the case studies and syndicate group work can get a bit much.

The great thing is that you can skip all that. Here's how to get the low-hanging fruit immediately.

But are you missing out? After all, surely all that stuff is there for a reason? I know you are ahead of the game and you don't want to be committed to certain dates and all that lecture-theatre stuff, but what about the interaction, the challenge, the deadlines, the performing under pressure?

You're right. You maybe are missing out a little. So here are some ideas on how you can get all the other good bits (apart from the content, of course) that exists on a traditional MBA without having to do one. Sneaky, huh?

■ Create individual modules with the best in the business. Once you have begun to identify the thought leaders whose ideas you really value and have read a couple of their books, do an Internet search to find out when they are next presenting in public and consider going to see them. You'll get their latest thinking, live is always more stimulating and you will probably be able to get one or two of your specific questions answered. Make an effort to go up at the end, shake hands and thank them for their efforts.

■ Email the guru. With any thought leaders whose ideas you admire: send an email and thank them. Some will respond and, although you wouldn't want to be overly demanding of their time, it helps build your network.

■ Learning budget. Decide to put aside 2% (at least) of your income into your personal training and development budget; this is to pay for anything which makes you even more effective than you currently are. Thus it could be for the gurus, or it could be for something quite different, such as going on a martial arts course or a drawing programme.

■ Build your network. Keep a note of all the great people you meet: be generous and help them out whenever and wherever you can. Over time you'll find your efforts get returned by the best people.

■ Coaching. Who would make a good coach for you? Is there someone in your business you could approach? Someone you could meet once a week for forty-five minutes who would be willing to challenge you? You won't know unless you ask, will you?

■ Brand name studies. Take a brand name, any big brand name: Starbucks, BA, Apple, whatever. Imagine you have been commissioned to come up with a pragmatic action-based list of twenty-five points to make the brand even stronger. Write a report. Get your coach to comment or book an hour with a strategy lecturer at your local university; get some feedback on your thoughts.

■ Library and online research. Ask if you can use the local university library: take a look at some of the research periodicals.

Here's an idea for you...

Decide to set up a learning team. You need three people who meet once a month for just an hour; ideally these people come from outside your main organisation. However, if that's all you have, don't delay: get started. Your simple goal is to enhance your own and each other's knowledge, skills and attitude. Each month bring along approximately ten minutes' worth of ideas or material, perhaps from a book or something like a great sale. Present and discuss it, taking a total of about twenty minutes. Then the other people have their turn to do the same. Start ringing and emailing to assemble the team right now.

- Proposing internally. Use the ideas that you learn about with your own business.
- Change champion. Become the champion for change you would like to see in others. Be a 'bit of a pain' at times, but make it happen.
- Subscribe to blogs. Discover the quality blogs in the fields of marketing and business planning, and take notes.
- Read widely. Follow up references to other books or studies.
- Learn another language. This will enhance your CV immediately; take some time off and learn in the country. If in any doubt, start with Spanish.
- Volunteer to lecture. Start with volunteering to speak at your local college or university, perhaps about your particular field or speciality. Do a good job and people will begin to ask for you.
- Start a blog. A blog is easy to start, cheap to begin and needn't be public until you are ready. It helps you gather your thoughts, on which you can seek feedback if you wish. It also allows you to gather materials for a possible book and it builds your brand. Are those enough reasons for you?
- Write some articles. As your personal thought leadership begins to develop, begin to write your own articles. Don't expect to be accepted for publication immediately; just keep writing and submitting. It will happen.

First, master your instrument. Then forget all that bullshit and play! Charlie Parker

How did it go?

Q. *Is all this extra stuff really necessary?*

A. Not essentially necessary, no – you can, of course, stay entirely book-based if you wish to do so. All of these ideas, though, will help turn concepts into reality, thoughts into action and reinforce the whole process. Do them if you possibly can.

Q. *Unfortunately where I work (which is partly the reason I am doing all this stuff), absolutely nobody is interested in starting a learning team. Any suggestions?*

A. Yes. Don't try and talk anyone into it. This may seem a surprising thing to say, but you want someone who, when you start explaining the idea, says 'yes, when do we start?' and not 'why would you want to do that?' You know the kind of thing. So just keep mentioning it to people and see who gets grabbed by the idea. People often say they can't find anyone, but then realise they are not actually doing any asking. Don't make assumptions, just explain the idea and the enthusiasts will come forward.

41

Instant MBA

42

11. Pricing – it depends how you look at it

How much for a coffee? It depends. How much for a bottle of water on a cold day in Moscow? On the edge of the Sahara? Quite. It's all about perception.

Pricing is no science; it's a beautiful art form. Come into the studio and learn the art of pricing.

Price and cost

Perhaps initially you feel that you should set a price which is dependent upon the cost of creating your product or service. So you take all the costs, the raw materials, salaries, transport, logistics, legal fees; anything and everything. And then you add the margin or profit you need to make – and there's the price! That seems pretty simple, doesn't it? Yes, and it is one way to do it, but it might lose you a lot of money; it might even destroy your business. More positively, it might be a huge missed opportunity. Read on…

Price and perception

The reason for this is that price is never an absolute thing. Price is as much about – if not all about – perception of value. Value is a very important term. What is your product or service worth to the buyer? This does not always correlate

Here's an idea for you...

I'd like you to do a little marketing survey. Ask twenty coffee drinkers about their coffee-buying habits. When they buy a cup of coffee on its own (i.e. not with a meal), how do they decide where to buy it? Try and establish all the variables; push beyond the quick response. For example if some people say 'price', ask them what price they pay – you may be surprised that many do not actually know. Hence they're not buying on price. They are buying on location, brand, fast response – things like that. How much of that information is transferable to your business or to your clients' businesses?

directly with costs. Some seats at the theatre are more expensive, and people will pay for them, because although the product (the play) is the same, certain seats are perceived to give you more value. In some areas a flat has a higher price than it would have elsewhere. The flat is exactly the same as a flat in another place, but this particular area is currently more fashionable and so the property has a higher price. What's the message: boost the perceived value and increase the price? Selling your cakes in a fancy box with a ribbon may allow you to significantly increase the price of the cakes. The essential message is that maybe you could be charging a lot more for your product or service already, or maybe just a little extra work could allow you to charge more in the near future… Certainly, talk less about cost and more about value.

Price and positioning

Price is one of the simplest ways to indicate to the prospect or customer where you are in the market. The consumer will position your price against others and will quickly understand whether you are meant to be cheap and cheerful or expensive and premium, or somewhere in between. Does your price express the right message?

Price and market penetration

Do you wish to price low and gain high market share and probable low margin (but a lot of low margins), or price high and take a nice fat margin and accept lower market share (but maybe from the customers who are easy to deal with)? This is a decision which needs to be taken.

Price and elasticity

Now, just so you are familiar with the jargon and can hold your own in a syndicate session, a price is elastic if it can be increased and little or nothing happens to consumer demand. It can be expressed mathematically but I'm certainly not going to go into that here. Bear this in mind, however.

Simply increase your prices until the customer says — no! Sir John Harvey Jones, from his programme *Troubleshooter*

How did it go?

Q. So – how do I set a price?

A. Begin by realising that the price you set is probably the strongest and most explicit piece of business and marketing communication about that product or service your company will release so it is worth considerable thought. Realise that getting it wrong could lose you a lot of money. Before you set the price you should answer the following questions: How much money do we want to make per sale? How much money do we have to make per sale? What are we trying to achieve with market share with this product? How will the price help us with this aim? What positioning messages versus the competition do we want the price to indicate? Are we being too nervous – could the price be higher with little reduction if any in sales? How elastic is the pricing?

Q. What about discounting and sales?

A. Simply remember that it's not quite as easy as you might think at first glance. For simplicity, let's say your product or service costs £50. You currently sell it at £100. That makes you £50. Not bad. OK, a tough customer beats you up at a negotiation and insists on 30% discount. You agree, that takes the price from £100 to £70. But what have you done to your margin? It was £50. It's now just £20; you've reduced your margin by 60%. Quite! Worth thinking about, isn't it? Make sure your sales and marketing teams know and abide by the rules on discounting, that you stick to them and you teach them how to negotiate. By the way, I accept that extra discount may get you extra business which may in turn reduce some costs or gain you market share. All well and good – but do the calculations before generalising about what a great deal you've just made.

12. Supermodels

Whatever way you look at it, a business course wouldn't be a business course without great models: triangles and 4 by 4 matrices and nested circles...

Sometimes it'll be all of those, inter-connected on an amazing PowerPoint slide. Let's get the essentials all covered.

A business model is a fast-track way of getting success. If someone is excellent at doing something they have an approach, they have a strategy. They may or may not be conscious of that approach but what other people can do is 'model' that approach – find out exactly what they are doing and attempt to replicate it. For instance, Michael Porter believes successful organisations build competitiveness in certain ways; how about if you copied those approaches? Here's another. Meredith Belbin's team model suggests that high-performance teams have certain combinations of players; how about if you ensured you had those in your team? You would up your chances of success, that's what.

Models are created through research and/or observation (such as those of Porter and Belbin) or intuition (Edward De Bono is a good example here). Either way they are ratified – or not – through ongoing use. Let's look in more detail at some useful examples.

Here's an idea for you...

You have fifteen minutes. Think of a client or, if you prefer, consider your own business. Identify your current business challenge. Take five minutes, no more. Think about your search criteria: make them as precise as possible. Now surf the net. Find a model which could help and read the ideas. Take five minutes, no more. Now identify the explicit actions you will take to overcome this challenge. Take five minutes. You guessed – no more. That's the power of the business model. Why reinvent excellence when you can pinch it from an established practitioner?

Belbin Team Inventory: team effectiveness

This was described by Dr Meredith Belbin after research at Henley Management College. The inventory assesses how an individual works in a team environment and thus can be helpful in producing a more effective team. The model identifies nine different team roles such as the Plant (creative and generator of ideas) and the Completer–Finisher (the perfectionist who makes things happen).

Boston Matrix from Boston Consulting Group: product analysis

This is a chart created by Bruce Henderson of the Boston Consulting Group for analysing product/business unit market share and growth rates. It articulates the well-known 'cash cow' term, which is a product or business unit that has zero or low maintained costs but still generates plentiful funds which can be used elsewhere in the business.

Maslow's Hierarchy of Needs: understanding personal motivation

Abraham Maslow identified that people tend to be motivated by different factors at various stages in their life. Thus, early in someone's career a big motivator is money. But perhaps later on, when money needs are essentially fulfilled, that person might wish to be more personally fulfilled – perhaps by making a contribution to society, or doing something similar. Understanding such motivations helps you release the best from both yourself and your employees.

Porter's Value Chain: competitive strategy

Michael Porter identified a chain of components from the birth of the product until it is in the hands of the customer. At each stage there is an opportunity to add value and hence build competitive differences.

Edward De Bono's Six Thinking Hats: creativity

De Bono realised people are not as creative as they might be because they get locked into their own personal mindset and also perhaps criticise others for changing mindset rather than just valuing an alternative viewpoint. He created six artificial hats which you can use in a meeting to formally describe when you are thinking in a particular way – for instance, De Bono's red hat is when you are 'being emotional', speaking from the heart and do not wish to be logical.

Where can you get a great model from? Now it's so easy – the Internet.

Change before you have to. Jack Welch

49

How did it go?

Q. Are models like these of any use in the real world?

A. In a word: yes. They give you a framework for thinking. Not because they will guarantee success, not because they will necessarily work and sometimes not because they are always all that good a model. But the answer is yes because they give you a framework for developing your own best ideas and they help you get ahead of the game. Use them for your own thinking; take time out and use a model to consider what needs to be done, when and how. At an awayday, introduce the ideas from a model to your team and ask them for their thoughts. You could also use them to introduce a vocabulary to your organisation so that instead of implicit statements about 'needing to be better' you could say 'we need more green hat [fresh start/creative, by the way] thinking' or 'we need to develop the service part of the value chain'.

Q. I've noticed that some business models contradict each other. All the gurus have their own particular thing. If I may be a little cynical here, too many of them seem to be 'flavour of the month' or a simple rehashing of something which is common sense. Wouldn't you agree?

A. There's a lot of truth in what you say. Consultants and/or gurus survive and thrive through their thoughts and trying to make their thoughts more important than those of anyone else. Brand new thoughts are rare; they tend to be evolutions, of course. Having said that, if you hear an idea repeated in many different ways but essentially saying the same thing it's probably a valuable idea which you should adopt. Then keep reading, because one of the other variations on a theme may work better for your service in your market. Stay open-minded about this; the bad ideas do not last long.

13. Know your thought leader 3: Tom Peters

Excellence! Love Peters or hate him, he's still banging away at a core idea: make excellence your minimum standard and you'll always be in demand. That's a nice position to be in.

Easy to say, but how's it done? And didn't many of those original In Search of Excellence case studies not do so well in the long term?

Tom Peters is the man who runs the Tom Peters Group (of course!). His main subject is excellence, on which he has written many influential books and articles. Importantly, though, he's not an academic and he isn't attached to any particular university. As well as being an author he spends a large part of his time on the lecture circuit. His most famous and probably most widely read book is *In Search of Excellence*. He is most definitely a key thought leader and you need to know about him.

What are his key ideas? Well, I immediately face a challenge: Peters has had a prolific output both in main texts but also via self-published mini-books and, most recently, his blog. In one sense (as his critics delight in pointing out) it's the same old messages every time – but the messages do shift subtly and often 'morph' into ones which are particularly relevant for our time.

Here's an idea for you...

Time to work on yourself. Take a sheet of paper and think about brands for a moment – high-street, international, local; it doesn't matter. Great ones will come to mind, but so will poor ones; don't discard the latter, just write them all down. What makes the great ones great? Try and come up with three factors, such as excellence of design, and imagine applying those factors to the weaker brands. Would they be transformed? And – this is the key – could those factors improve your team, your company or even your personal brand?

It can also be emphasised that although 'excellence' is now perhaps an over-used word, it certainly wasn't in the context in which Peters first used it – customer service – twenty-six years ago. Peters also pioneered the thinking behind design as a differentiator (Apple, Starbucks) and the importance (indeed the existence) of the women's market. He may drive you mad with his rants but he is worth keeping tabs on. And he does tend to walk his talk; he works to high standards and is immediately accessible – for free – via his blog.

A few years ago Peters assembled a summary book to celebrate his sixtieth birthday called *60 TIBS (Things I Believe)*. Reviewing some of these is one of the best and quickest ways to access his thinking.

■ TIB 1 'Technicolour rules! Passion moves mountains!'
   That's classic Tom Peters: great businesses have energy, show energy and are passionate about what they do. His fans love this stuff. Of course, many academics hate it – where's the data, where's the research, they ask. Think about it. Where would you generally rather stay? In a hotel where the staff are responsive and friendly and show passion or in one where the service metrics are at 88%? Quite. Maybe Peters has a point.

- TIB 3 Revolution rules. Most of the strategy guys are preaching this message, but Peters is direct: 'If you choke on the word revolution, I am fearful for your future'. Reinvent, and do it regularly, he says.
- TIB 10 Big Stinks (mostly). '…truth is, Big Company performance has always been more problematic than imagined and most adventures in consolidation fail miserably.' Peters reminds us that great companies tend to start small and often lose their greatness when they get large. The reason is logical: they lose their agility.
- TIB 14 Forget it. Be a constant, continuous learner. Of all the thought leaders, Peters is the strongest on learning and relearning. He's often harsh on the MBA curriculum arguing that it needs to cover more of the 'soft' stuff. To Peters, 'soft is hard and hard is soft'.
- TIB 19 Action takes precedence. Get on with it. If there is a danger with the MBA and, in fact, with too much academic thinking, it's the paralysis of analysis.
- TIB 27 Women rule. Tom Peters has been one of the strongest proponents of reminding both men and women of the high value of women in business.
- TIB 31 Design – the new seat of the soul. It's worked brilliantly for Apple, Starbucks, Innocent Juices: the sheer desire of great design. It need not be expensive, either.
- TIB 43 It's a brand new, brand you world. Whether you like it or not, you have a brand. It's what people say about you when you're not there.
- TIB 46 Excellence is a state of mind. As Peters sometimes puts it: one-minute excellence is a decision to be excellent.

■ TIB 52 Avoid the epitaph from hell. Peters asks, 'Do you want an epitaph that runs along the lines of "I would have done great stuff but my boss wouldn't let me."?'

So what do we learn from Peters? Let's sum up.

1. Passion is a business possibility. It'll make people buy from you and make work more enjoyable.
2. Reinvent or die.
3. Small still is beautiful.
4. Be a learner.
5. Don't just talk: walk.
6. There are forgotten and underestimated markets out there: the women's market is the biggest.
7. Design is not a luxury, it's an essential.
8. Work on your brand.
9. Excellence is a choice.
10. Don't come up with excuses.

Read odd stuff. Look anywhere for ideas.

Tom Peters

How did it go?

Q. *I want an excellent company. Peters almost provides too many ideas, so how do I create one?*

A. Use the ten-point summary list above and read his blog regularly. After a week or two you will soon appreciate which ideas might work for you. Above all – if you really are to follow Peters – you must act.

Q. *Isn't it true that most of the companies in Peters' original study – In Search of Excellence – have gone bust?*

A. No. That's a bit of an urban myth, probably encouraged by his detractors. Given that it's some twenty-six years since it was published, the fundamental ideas are still as sound as ever. Clearly the companies have changed, but that's evolution.

14. Vision

Step back for a moment and make sure you're up and running on one of the basics of business – the importance of a vision and how to implement that vision.

Here's how to get beyond that predictable 'to be the no. 1... in...' and create a vision which inspires both staff and customers.

What a vision statement actually is, and why it matters

Your vision statement is typically a statement which is visible to both customers and staff alike. It is visible in the office, on the shop floor, on PowerPoint slides and in reports. It is a statement of intent, a 'where we want to be' expression. A true vision statement also tends to indicate an expression of the organisation's values. It's a reference point for when views diverge, a standard to which to aspire and a touchstone for what you are trying to do. It should provide guidance on issues such as ways to behave, what direction to take and ultimately what kind of organisation you wish to become. If done well, it can really help your organisation's success.

Make no mistake, you need one. And even if you are a one-man band and probably won't be sharing it with anyone, it's worth doing the exercise of drawing one up. If you feel it's difficult or hard to define, that may be a concerning sign about your business, perhaps showing that it lacks real focus and/or distinction.

Vision and mission

Strictly speaking, a vision statement is not the same as a mission statement. But, as with so many of these terms, where there's a lack of understanding they tend to be used interchangeably. When determining your vision statement it is certainly worth striving for the strict meaning, which is a clear statement of intent, to define what the organisation is about.

Creating your vision statement

There are some clear stages to go through.

1. Define the mission; this normally revolves around your core competence, i.e. the thing which makes you different. For a publisher it might be 'to become the publisher of choice in the field of new author science fiction novels in Europe through innovation of story and quality of writing'.
2. Define your values, such as 'innovation'.
3. And hence define your vision: 'As a publisher we ensure a choice of high-quality innovative science fiction writing for those living in Europe'.

Too often vision and/or mission statements become blurred in meaning or generic (e.g. 'to be the publisher of choice' or 'to be the no. 1 in science fiction'). The difficulty with these is that if they are not credible or appropriately inspirational (not everyone can be no. 1, after all) they will be seen as meaningless. And, being pragmatic for a moment, 'being no. 1' doesn't necessarily mean being the most successful, wealthy or even having the most fun.

Here's an idea for you...

If you've already got a vision statement get your team together and create another statement from scratch; ignore anything you have at present. Go through the whole process. If you end up with what you have now, that's probably a good sign. If you end with something different, it's great that you did the exercise. Whatever you end up with, ensure it is communicated as quickly as possible to the whole organisation.

57

Now, it's not hard to create these statements, but what you want is a great one. And a great one is one which inspires you to stay focused and do the best. That is created by putting more quality time into the process. Also, get everyone's buy-in. Ensure that everyone comes to the planning session, that the 'quiet' ones get their say, and don't fall into the trap of statements which sound good but which are difficult to understand if you are in, say, accounts.

Implementing your statement
Use it everywhere: in reception, on reports, at the bottom of recruitment advertisements. Help each department understand how the statement relates to them (for instance, how those in the warehouse can help a retailer become great at customer service). Explain it to customers as well. Review it every year in the planning round and be proud of it – and if you aren't, develop one which you are proud of.

Here are some real examples.
- Sainsbury's: Our mission is to be the consumer's first choice for food, delivering products of outstanding quality and great service at a competitive cost through working 'faster, simpler and together.'
- Apple: Apple continues to lead the industry in innovation with its award-winning desktop and notebook computers, OS X operating system, and iLife and professional applications.
- Wal-Mart: To give ordinary folk the chance to buy the same thing as rich people.
- Walt Disney: To make people happy.

Make a dent in the universe. Steve Jobs

How did it go?

Q. We've had a vision statement for a long time, but nobody believes in it. How can we make it useful?

A. This in many ways is *the* question. Firstly remind yourself and the rest of the leadership team why it might be useful to have one. Then book an awayday and go through the process of creating the statement from scratch. If you do that, you will come up with something that is useful. The bottom line: ditch what you have now if it isn't working.

Q. I was once told mission was about 'now' and vision was 'future'. How come your definition is different?

A. You're correct, that is one definition, although it is the minority one. As always, come back to what is useful for you. These statements are really about direction and focus. You can consider separately, in your marketing planning, what kind of organisation you want to be now and in the future.

15. Human resources

Ugh! Don't you hate that term? Let's get back to people – how to find them, keep them and motivate them.

It's been said many times of course: people are your greatest asset, but you'll also be aware — being truthful — that they can also be your greatest nightmare!

Essentially, you want to do three things with people. Firstly, find the best; secondly, get the best out of the best; thirdly, keep the best doing their best. You'll notice that that challenge gets harder from first to second to third, so let's take a look at each of those challenges in turn.

Finding the best

Whatever business you are in (or in which you are advising/consulting) – service or manufacturing, high tech or low tech, sweet shop or call centre – the business is the sum of the people in it. So you need to have the best and that starts with getting the best.

Begin by making this a core activity in the organisation. Make everyone keen to find the best people to work alongside them. Create a simple reward scheme for finding good employees. After all, those who already work in an organisation tend to know what sort of people are good for that organisation; it can also be a lot cheaper than a big recruitment campaign. And however wonderful HR are, they often don't fully understand all the roles in an organisation. Any other recruitment process should be subsidiary to this 'people find people' process.

Secondly, ensure that any contact with your organisation can allow those who are impressed with you to enquire about positions which are vacant. Thus it should be clear wherever you have a presence – on your website/blog, at an exhibition, on any publications – what someone should do if they're interested in joining you.

Once the organisation lives and breathes the concept of 'everybody recruits', you need to be clear on what the best actually is. Consider three factors: knowledge, skills and attitude. For any person you seek, define those three aspects of the job: the knowledge (what they need to know), the skills (what they must be able to carry out with consistent competence) and finally attitude (the way they think). Remember that ease of trainability is generally considered to be in the order of knowledge, then skills, and then attitude – and yet too little time is often given to seeking someone with the appropriate attitude. Knowledge can be the easiest to develop, but people are often recruited on the basis of just that; consider giving more attention to finding people with the right attitude instead.

Get the best out of the best

Once you have the best on board, how do you get them to consistently deliver their best? Begin by ensuring that they go through an induction programme. At the very least this should equip them with whatever they need to do their job on a daily basis. It will also introduce them to names and faces so they can ask the right people for

Here's an idea for you...

Take five people in your team (or one of your client's teams). What motivates each of those people now? What do you believe will be motivating them in eighteen months' time? The same factors or something different? What does that imply for the way you currently manage and lead them?

61

help when necessary. What are known as 'hygiene factors' should be sorted out. Will they be paid on time? Do they have a computer? A desk? An email account? A job description? Then check that they know their objectives and how they are being measured. Finally, make sure they get things like positive reinforcement and appropriate praise. Are you reinforcing the best by catching them doing things right?

Keep the best doing their best

You got the best on board, you stopped them getting dulled and cynical within the first few weeks. How do you get them to perform to their best for several years at least? By understanding what motivates them, which is not the same for all people all of the time, or for an individual all of the time. You intuitively know that. Most of us want money, but money rarely compensates for a job we hate, so there must be more to it. Abraham Maslow developed a model called the 'hierarchy of needs' which details the items we all require to keep us motivated. At the bottom of the hierarchy are the basics – food and shelter – in the middle are growth and challenge and at the top is 'self-actualisation' or 'being the best version of ourselves'. Can you help people be the best version of themselves? If you can, they'll stick with you. If you can't – well, at best they will be dulled, at worst they will leave.

People are not lazy. They simply have impotent goals — that is, goals that do not inspire them.

Anthony Robbins, from a seminar

How did it go?

Q. How do you retain an outstanding employee who says you have nothing more to offer?

A. Try and get out of the office to some neutral ground. Go to a café or go on a walk and ask this person what they are really looking for, what they feel a new employer will offer them. Listen carefully, don't get defensive and get beyond any quick responses like 'they'll give me more challenge'. Ask for forty-eight hours to see if you can come up with anything. If you can, great; if you can't, stay on amicable terms and remind your employee that they are welcome back if it doesn't work out; people do often return and bring extra experience with them. If they are leaving after a short period of time because they felt unfulfilled, that was possibly bad recruitment or bad management or both and needs to be addressed.

Q What do you do when a person is not performing as you wish them to perform?

A. Go back to basics. Do they know what they are meant to be doing or has it become assumed? Once their objectives are explicit, do they have the knowledge and skills to do the job? If they have and are still not performing it has become (probably) a disciplinary issue and your HR team should be involved.

16. Stop advertising and start telling stories

You know much of advertising is just pure bullshit and you don't believe it, so why should your customers believe your messages?

Start telling stories, especially stories which spread.

The challenge

Potential customers are now very sophisticated and getting more so by the day. They are also constantly distracted with alternative demands on their time. How on earth do you influence them?

In the Old World of Work, the audience was less sophisticated, less distracted and not already overloaded with stuff (products and services). In the New World of Work, the audience is very sophisticated (the Internet allows anyone to become an expert at anything within minutes, whether it is how pensions are calculated or the side effects of drugs). It is also highly distracted and interruption-driven (iPods in ears, texting, running to a meeting…) and with more than enough stuff (from shoes to mobile phones) to keep anyone going for decades.

For a marketer this latter situation is a potential nightmare. If you can't get people's attention, you can't sell to them. And if you can't sell, they can't buy. And if they don't buy, you don't have a viable business.

Here's an idea for you...

Choose either you or one of your clients. I'll assume it's you. What's special about what you do? Think of a customer or client who has really appreciated that speciality you have. Maybe they told you or dropped you an email or you have just heard bits of the episode from various members of the team. Now grab your laptop, or a bit of paper and a pencil will suffice. Write a 100-word story to encapsulate it and make the incident real.

An approach...

So how do you sell in the New World of Work? The answer is to let the audience spread the message, then it will be both trusted and carried directly to its intended audience. But why would they pass on your message? Because it is engaging, it means something to them and ultimately it gives hope. It's a perfect story. Here are some great 'perfect story' tellers:

- Volvo. The story is safety. The hope is driving without undue danger.
- Innocent Juices. The story is young start-up company makes good. The hope is health.
- John Lewis. The story is there is another way of doing business. The hope is that it'll be easy to shop.
- Starbucks. The story is 'a third place'. The hope is a small escape, a little luxury.
- The city of San Francisco. The story is a magical place. The hope is a city without the ravages of globalisation.
- Apple. The story is your destiny. The hope is you manage it: you make the choices.

Now here are some who are getting better at storytelling:
- BUPA. No longer about illness and health checks, but about wellness and quality of life.
- Business schools. No longer about an MBA qualification but about building your brand.

■ Guardian newspapers. No longer (just) news which is available anywhere, but an amazing online resource for an equally amazing lifestyle.

There are those who remain remarkably poor at storytelling…
■ Most governments. What is the story? Where is the hope?
■ IBM. Huh? Exactly.

What do the great storytellers have in common? Although they will advertise, the advertisement is just to feed the stories. For example, Volvo loves 'case studies' (e.g. how their safety systems have saved lives), Innocent Juices wants you to drop in and look around, Starbucks wants you to know all about their coffee growers. The main way they sell is by the message being a great story which is then spread 'meme like'. The term 'meme' was coined by biologist Richard Dawkins to parallel the term gene. It is defined as a unit of information which is transmitted from mind to mind. The classic example is a catchy tune. Ideally you want your story to be so good that it becomes a meme, like the Cadbury Gorilla. What do I mean? You'd better get on the Internet quick!

The point of any story can penetrate deeper than the point of any bullet.

Lawrence Nault, *The Mountain Hermit*

How did it go?

Q. Neither I nor my team have really done storytelling since school! So how exactly do I create a story?

A. That's no bad thing; forget school. Think films instead. What do the films you find most satisfying have? Clear starts and endings, there was closure, the film was probably optimistic, too – people like hope from their stories. You were engaged and gripped: what was going to happen next? There may have been a car chase, a sex scene along the way. That's the way you create a great story. Whether you are selling plumbing services (in which case the story starts with the drama of a leaking roof and ends up with a relieved young couple dragging out a sofa to dry…) or consultancy services, you are the film director and you must create a great story.

Q. If everyone's telling stories they'll have the same level of impact as a mailshot – not much. How do I keep my stories fresh?

A. Stories have been told since the start of time. You keep a story fresh by making it relevant. If you're in an insurance company and you know that your point of relevance is responsiveness when a client needs to make a claim, that's what you tell in your story. You keep your story fresh by ensuring it is real, by using real characters and real events. Tell the story of two holidaymakers who lost everything in Singapore; you got them back home, safely, all expenses paid. Keep it real and relevant.

17. Planning and strategy

How to plan in a world of rapid change, and how to create a winning strategy when there is no winning strategy.

Strategy was once the 'big thing' of the MBA programme: where is it now?

It's still there because it's still needed. The problem is that the stability of which strategy (and by the way, I'm defining strategy as a long-term plan which has a definite goal or outcome in mind; it tends to be high level and is distinguished from tactics which are the details of making that strategy happen) is so desirous, has disappeared for so many businesses in so many markets. Retail, manufacturing, tourism, publishing, schools: you name it, it's a very different world now.

Strategy is often associated with the game of chess and some have suggested the game was an early strategy modeller for battle – who knows? But imagine this. You are playing a game of chess; you have a great strategy and it is slowly but surely playing out. You are highly likely to win, when suddenly a toddler rushes in from another room and hurls the board onto the floor. Clearly your strategy is ruined; after all, you need a certain stability for a strategy to get an opportunity to work. In the Old World of Work, that was often the case; here are some instances:

- IBM: Nobody ever got fired for buying IBM.
- Building Society: you can't trust (or even get) a mortgage from elsewhere.
- M&S: if we don't want to accept credit cards, we won't.

Here's an idea for you...

Take your business. Take a couple of your competitors. Finally take a few companies who have some similarities, maybe size or geography or business model. Be absolutely ruthless. What are they doing that you believe makes them successful and that you are *not* doing, what ways of working could you learn from them? Whether it's a coffee shop being open at 6.30 a.m. instead of 8.00 a.m., a publisher running a blog giving free chapter samples or a dentist offering the first inspection free – it's worth trying. Identify five immediate 'modelling excellence' actions that you can take.

In the New World of Work the upsets are more frequent, much more rapid and harder to anticipate – even more, sometimes, than a toddler bursting into the room.

- Microsoft: software becomes more important than hardware once you have a common operating system.
- Kodak: what happened to film sales? Where did they go overnight?
- Tesco: yes, we are only a supermarket, but we are going to start a bank.

There are three fundamentals to consider:

1. From where do you get great strategies?
- Thought leaders, by reading the thoughts and works of those who spent 90% of their time in the field – Michael Porter, Gary Hamel, Tom Peters, etc. For these guys it is their life's work and passion to know what makes organisations tick and keep them ticking. On initial reading it appears that they all are different, even conflicting. But no: read deeply and you will find that their ideas align. And that is what you are looking for, of course: the fundamental truths, the points which you will cover as you do your own MBA.
- Modelling excellence and becoming your own thought leader. How does a great thought leader work? They model excellence: they notice what creates success and what is replicable. You can do the same. What is working for your competitors or for organisations of your size? Try it.

■ Incremental improvement, doing more of the same. You are successful; maybe you would like to be more so? Identify the small or large aspects of the way you operate that are attractive to customers or which attract great staff, and do more of them.

2. How do you cope with a lack of stability which reduces the opportunities to 'unfold' a strategy?

■ Act quickly. A differentiator which you must implement as quickly as possible is the ability to be responsive. As your organisation gets bigger, the danger is that you get slower.

■ Pre-select rapid strategies; go for those which are simple rather than complex.

3. How do you turn a strategy into a plan, into something which actually happens?

■ Project management. Few organisations invest formally in true project-management skills. Test it; ask for definitions of what a critical path is, for example – you'll get all kinds of vague answers! And that's worrying, because if you are not managing your critical path, you are not managing your route to business.

■ Communication. Find a great way to communicate. Here's one idea which works: a rolled-out monthly report. Once a month all managers meet and are briefed by the board at 9.00 a.m. At 11.00 a.m. those managers meet with their team leaders and brief them. At 2.00 p.m. those team leaders brief the people who report to them.

You can have the greatest strategy in the world but what is the point if no one cares?

Patrick Dixon, *Building a Better Business*

How did it go?

Q. As an organisation, I genuinely feel we are unique. And, to be honest, I want to be unique – so where do I find a strategy?

A. As a 'package', I'm sure that you are unique. But when you look at the various aspects of your business – logistics, marketing, etc. – there will be people in the same business as you. Learn from them. Was Starbucks unique when it started? Yes, but it can still learn from McDonald's, both the good and the bad…

Q. If strategy is so brilliant, why do so few organisations appear to have one or fail to execute their strategy?

A. Well, largely because strategy is generally put forward by those who have an academic background and are immersed in research and theory, and yet strategy needs to be executed by sharp-end practitioners. Find someone in your organisation who can act as translator between the two, or find a friend at a local university who is willing to help you with that translation exercise in return for perhaps using you as a case study.

18. Know your thought leader 4: Peter Drucker

The 'grand old man', sadly no longer with us, and a prolific writer. If I only had about 1000 words (and I do, actually), what would you need to know from him – and what can you use?

Don't worry, I'll give it to you! And, more importantly, I'll show you how you can use it in your own business or to advise your clients on what's important.

So, who was Peter Drucker? He had four main roles: he was a lecturer at a university, a management consultant, an author and a columnist; many a sound bite is attributed to him. Throughout his long life he remained exceedingly active even until his last days and was a particularly prolific writer and thought generator. Unlike many other thought leaders his legacy is less a particular book than two important concepts: the knowledge worker and management by objectives. He is most definitely a key thought leader to include as you get to grips with your MBA.

Here's an idea for you...

Consider your business; if you're consulting, do this for a client. Rate yourself between one to ten, where one is appalling and ten is outstanding, on these aspects. Firstly, motivating your knowledge workers (i.e. getting them to provide of their best and feel valued, having low staff turnover). Then, providing great leadership (i.e. teams knowing what they are meant to be doing, catching people doing things right). Next, keeping the business simple so that it's fast and responsive, and finally regularly reinventing it (with 'that's the way we've always done things' treated with suspicion). If they're not coming in at ten, what action can you take?

Over a long and active lifetime, Drucker covered many areas. Here are some of the most significant, which many people in many different organisations – public and private – have found both interesting and useful.

The knowledge worker

Drucker appears to have created the term 'knowledge worker' and a considerable interest of his was the emergence of a new breed of worker for whom ideas and brain work were more important than 'products'. Drucker – who was born in 1909 – was ideally suited to see this tendency shift and accelerate during his lifetime. He recognised that knowledge workers would need to be managed in different ways to other kinds of employees, given that ideas are produced in a very different way to a product.

■ Action point: Work out how you are motivating your knowledge workers.

MBO: management by objectives

Drucker was a clear and structured thinker. He was brilliant at getting to the heart of the matter and, not surprisingly, wanted management to be the same. His suggestion was that managers should set measurable objectives which employees would agree to and then perform against – then both managers and team members would know exactly where they stood. The term SMART (specific, measurable, agreed, realistic, timely) has become popular for helping to create specificity in an objective.

■ Action point: Ensure everyone has measurable objectives.

Simplicity

This is not a term you will find Drucker uses in his works particularly (in general, he did not share the current fad for trying to 'brand' any idea or theory), but he certainly was someone who liked to keep things simple and did not like unnecessary jargon – or the term 'guru' which was frequently applied to him. Once he famously scolded an audience for saying his lecture had been wonderful. He reminded them that this was not the measure of its effect; the measure was what they actually did.

■ Action point: Don't hide behind complexity or complex initiatives; keep it simple.

Reinvention

Drucker was not at all nostalgic. He was a forward thinker – marvellously so, as he continued to consult and lecture into his nineties. He was also one of the first to recognise that however successful a business might be, that very success might eventually be its downfall if it meant the business could not reinvent itself as times and markets changed around it.

■ Action point: Ensure your business is sufficiently fluid, so that it stays every bit as nimble as a small start-up company.

Management is doing things right; leadership is doing the right things. Peter Drucker

How did it go?

Q. Was Drucker correct?

A. Well, on what? Drucker was unlike many thought leaders or gurus in that he didn't have just 'one big thing' which he kept pushing; there are many aspects to his work. If he did have a big thing at all, it was developing an amazing 'science' of managing and leading people. Drucker clearly used examples and models which defended his points; who doesn't? However, large numbers of people running and leading organisations all over the world have found that Drucker's work can give them an interesting and useful structure for their thinking. Drucker also had the benefits of clear, insightful thinking himself and a reluctance to wrap simple ideas up in unnecessary 'guru jargon'. When the jury comes in, the overall verdict will be that Drucker's ideas do actually work. Use them.

Q. I have heard criticisms of MBO, management by objectives. Has it fallen out of favour?

A. No, and it is good that you raise the issue. The point is that management and/or leadership is not only MBO. That was the mistake some practitioners were making; setting objectives and then leaving their people to it. Not the right idea at all. MBO was simply adding refinements to a process that should have been in place anyway: knowing your people, matching task to person, coaching, briefing, reviewing and inspiring. Instead MBO should fit into a bigger picture and when it does, it is highly successful. Mortar is brilliant, but it needs the bricks.

19. Good is simply no longer good enough!

What raising standards really means...

In a market which is increasingly open and increasingly global, businesses simply have to be better and good is no longer good enough.

In business, how good do you have to be? Better than the competition? Well, of course. If you have no competition, then your standards can be as low as you like; after all, your customers have no other place they can go. In the Old World of Work, pre-globalisation, pre-ease of comparison and communication via the Internet, you may not have had any competition in your town or city or country and that meant, in reality, that you had no competition at all. But in the New World of Work, everyone is your competitor.

So, what's to be done? Raise your standards. Ah – but how do you do that? Firstly, understand the scale of standards. Your organisation has a certain competence, talent, ability, call it what you will. Use it, 'squeeze it to the max', whatever that might be. But you can multiply its effectiveness many times by your decisions. And one decision is to raise your standards.

Here's an idea for you...

Take your job (receptionist or team leader or credit controller or…), your team (internal sales, media production, whatever), division (manufacturing, HR) or company. Write a brief 100-word story entitled 'This is what it would take for me or my team or my division or my organisation to be considered absolutely, truly, amazing!' Then review that story and identify two actions. And take them – today. Where's your mobile?

Here's my standards scale: Dire, poor, OK, good, very good, excellent, outstanding, awe-inspiring. Imagine an organisation working at each of those standards. What will happen to it? Short term? Long term? Think it through before you read on.

Well, here's what happens.

■ If your organisation is dire, you'll be out, bankrupt, no more, and that will happen pretty well immediately. There is no long term if dire is the operating standard.

■ If the organisation works at poor, it may take a little longer for people to catch up with you, but you'll be out of business once they realise what you are up to and the way they are being treated. Once again there is no long term for you, not if your operating standard is poor.

■ If you choose to be OK, then you're fine for the short term, and if you are willing to raise your standards you have a long-term future. But bear in mind that you can't simply stay at OK. Who wants to buy from someone who is 'OK'? They will wish to go to someone who is good, or someone who is very good. They'll go to someone who is excellent. And who, for that matter, simply wants to be just OK? There is no long-term future in that.

■ If you are good, then people will be interested in buying from you both in the short term and long term. You should be able to hang on to some customers, but will you be able to keep them and develop them? They may start going to an organisation who is better; you see, good is no longer good enough. Certainly not in the long term. But, hopefully, if you are good you are also good enough to recognise the need to raise your standards.

- How about if you are very good? Now you're talking. People are much more interested in you. There are more possibilities open to you. Customers are keen to work with you. It is easier to defend your prices.
- What about if you are excellent? Fantastic. There are never, ever enough excellent companies about the place. You'll be in demand, you'll always be doing well.
- Could your business step up to outstanding? Of course it could. Because you've got the message, haven't you? Every one of these steps is a choice. Your talent is recruited and developed, but your standards are a choice. And if you were outstanding, think of what would be open to your organisation.
- If you were awe-inspiring there would be absolutely no stopping your business. How about it? Make that decision today and simply decide to be awe-inspiring. They'll be after you; you can name your price.

And how do you do it? Create a team of passionate people to go through your organisation, top to bottom, bottom to top, side to side. Get them to examine every process – the way bills are paid, phones are answered, innovations are captured, sales are celebrated, complaints are recorded, products are built, training is held. Make every single process better. It may take weeks, months, possibly even a year. But from the day you start your competitiveness is soaring, so do start.

Good isn't good enough any more. Seth Godin

How did it go?

Q. But surely this is a never-ending treadmill. Isn't very good today only OK in two years' time?

A. Yes, you're absolutely correct. And you can either see that as a threat – 'how will we ever get better than we are now…?'– or you can see it as an opportunity that your competitors will ignore because they have got comfortable. Think *kaizen*, the Japanese word for never-ending improvement: improve your product, your service, your attitude, your logistics, your payment terms, your warranty, your range of colours. But above all, improve your standards.

Q. Don't we need some people just to be workers and allow others to be chiefs?

A. That's not the point! A 'worker' can be excellent, a 'chief' can be OK. The point is that everyone must strive for excellence to create a competitive organisation, but the choice of the standard at which they operate is not a function of job title or experience or pay. It is a personal choice. Good leadership will instil the message that excellent people make an excellent organisation. And why should an individual choose to be excellent? Well, it guarantees their employability in their chosen career, and that's a very nice position to be in.

20. New World of Work drivers 1: acceleration

Here's the first detailed look at the background to the new management, leadership and strategy practices which are needed in the New World of Work.

But in a subtly different way. Read on.

The context

Let's look at the term 'the New World of Work' which came into being about ten years ago, and is to be distinguished from the Old World of Work (work before the general occurrence of email, if you like). There are seven drivers of change which have caused a significant change in the way we work, and the first one is acceleration. There is no disagreement with the statement that change has always been happening; this terminology is simply concerned with the rate of change and the fact that the current and growing rate of change has imposed further changes upon certain practical human physiological parameters (in particular thinking speed and personal resilience).

Acceleration

Acceleration is a term used to define the rate of change. I disagree with those who say that human beings do not like change. No, we do: new films, new books, even new jobs. Even the most conservative MD is willing to change his tie once in a while. This is about rate of change, the sheer exhausting rate of change.

Here are some examples of what I mean. It has been said that world knowledge is currently doubling every five years, but by the year 2018 it will be doubling every seventy-three days. In the 1960s many people kept their jobs for twenty-three years or

Here's an idea for you...

Go on a walk and do nothing – no phone, no cup of coffee, no chat, no cigarette, no newspaper. Feeling anxious already? Do you think you can do it? Just walk for ten minutes. Then think about it. If, like most people, you find it caused you to be a bit anxious, it'll remind you how addicted you have become to activity. Do that ten-minute walk on regular basis.

more; now it's more likely to be just over two years. In the seventeenth century, there would have been as much new information for an educated person to acquire in the whole of their lifetime as there is for us in just a single day. Internet search engines allow random bits of information to be assembled almost instantly which would have taken teams of people weeks to assemble in the past…

And here's the problem. The rate of change is now faster than our speed of thinking. Once – in the Old World of Work – humans were the fastest thing around. Now we are too damn slow.

Implications for organisations

Think about the relentless drive for efficiency as opposed to being effective. Are you wondering what the difference is? Try this story. A group of managers was travelling through the jungle. The jungle was dense; the managers had been in it for many months. A routine had been established: get up early, spend the day hacking through the jungle, set up camp, cook the evening meal, sleep, get up and do it again. And again. To break the monotony there were occasional training courses on how to sharpen the machetes and sometimes even new machetes would arrive by FedEx. But basically things were much the same. In fact, most of the managers no longer knew where they were and what they were trying to do. They just seemed to have one mission in life: to keep hacking through the jungle.

Of course, occasionally people asked questions, sometimes when tramping along, especially after another weird lunch of baked snake or after supper around the fire when faces were hidden in the shadow. In the end, it always came back to the reply 'we're making progress', and the official number of kilometres covered would be read out. It was always impressive.

One morning, very early, a young manager decided he'd had enough and decided to climb and climb high. He chose a tree carefully and exchanged his boots for trainers. He left his pack on the ground and just strapped a bottle of water to his belt. It was tough: the canopy was dense and at every level there were different insects, birds and monkeys which startled him. But as he climbed, the air was definitely getting cleaner, the light was looking brighter and suddenly he had a glorious experience: he broke through the canopy. There was a glorious rising sun. But he was startled and shouted to his colleagues who were starting to set off. At first they couldn't hear him, but at last they heard his words loud and clear: 'Wrong jungle!'

You get the point, of course: that 'organisation' had become very efficient. But, given they were in the wrong jungle, they were not very effective.

Implications for you

You must slow down to the speed of thought, again. There is nothing wrong with a mobile phone, a BlackBerry – but these devices can actually lower creativity and hence innovation. They can increase your stress and make you less intelligent in your decision making. Choose to deliberately slow down to the speed of your greatest asset: your thinking.

If things seem under control, you are just not going fast enough. Mario Andretti

83

How did it go?

Q. I'm a cynic: surely previous generations complained about rate of change and speed, too. Are we really so different?

A. You are, of course, correct; there were complaints about speed and change in the past. But I'm highlighting one big difference. Our greatest asset – our speed of thinking – has been affected. We do not have time to think because we are being bombarded from all directions. We're the first generation to have to really suffer from this bewildering experience.

Q. I really do buy into your ideas, but I work in an organisation full of manic BlackBerry-picking and phone-hugging junkies. What can I do?

A. Don't join the addicted crew. Stop more; think more and be more. Notice who is actually more effective, who has fewer tantrums, who gets home on time, who suffers from less stress and who addresses the real priorities. Then maybe one or two of them will learn from you – I can but hope…

21. Don't be aloof: learn how to sell

It's the one thing which never gets properly covered in the business school modules and yet it's the one thing which is essential to a successful business: how to sell.

I'll make sure you can do it — and you'll even enjoy it.

What's the problem here? Well, essentially the problem is that too many people are not willing to get their hands dirty, to do some real selling… Everyone loves the intellectual nature of strategic planning, the glamour of marketing, but selling? Where's the skill in that?

That's the thing, actually. When you are selling, you soon find out whether your strategies are worth the paper they are written on because you get your results immediately: sale or no sale. No hiding behind long-term market penetration plans or behind things like 'awaiting the output of the product focus groups'. This is where the rubber hits the road.

Do be clear, because this is important. You can absorb all the ideas in the world from your MBA but if you can't sell – whether it's an idea, a product, why you should get a job or a pay rise or a relocation to the Maldives – you will not be as successful as you would wish. But it's really easy. Forget the myths about obscure techniques and closing, here's what you actually need to do.

■ More ask, less tell. Whoever you are selling to, talk to them and find out what they really want and why it is important to them. Before you state your salary request at the job interview, find out how important this role is to your possible employers. When you ask, you get people to think. Too much telling simply puts people into a trance (you remember those lectures, surely!) which is not a great environment for selling. Ask more, tell less.

■ More reasons, fewer bullets. Once you know what your customers want, give them nice logical reasons why you are the person or the company to provide it. Think about what's in it for them and forget the streams of bullets in your brochure. Tell them what's relevant and forget the rest.

■ More conversation, less PowerPoint. Keep your laptop in your bag; you may never need to take it out. Talk to customers instead; build rapport, understand their concerns and worries. Show them that it's their meeting and not just another call on your agenda.

■ More them, less you. Talking about yourself is easy, but they either know about you or will do so soon. What they are concerned about is whether you understand them and their needs, so show them you do.

Here's an idea for you...

Take a product and list some of its features such as 'it comes in red', 'service is free', etc. What does that feature mean to the potential purchaser? The fact that it comes in red means that buyers could create a real splash of colour. Free service means they could buy with confidence knowing they'd have no post-sales concerns. You've just created advantages which mean… well, being able to create a splash of colour means brightening up a home; having no post-sales concerns means shopping online is a pleasure. You've just created benefits. Facts or features do not necessarily sell, but advantages and benefits do.

- More decisions, fewer meetings. Keep getting decisions. Ask if things make sense, whether that is a good idea, do they have a budget? You have a right to know that stuff, so ask; otherwise you will end up in loads of meetings and chasing telephone calls.
- More concerns, less avoiding realities. Find out why they haven't given you an order rather than assuming it will happen at some time.
- More lock in, less generic. Show them you are special, so they can't go elsewhere. And create lots of reasons why you are special.
- More urgency, less 'any time'. Give them reasons to act; you don't want to still be speaking to them about this bit of business in a year's time.

I sell ice in the winter, I sell fire in hell / I am a hustler, baby, I'll sell water to a well...

Jay-Z

How did it go?

Q. How do you sell when your competition is cheaper than you? My major competitor is bigger – probably always will be – and has greater buying power. It's had several years of eating up market share and has strong brand presence. How can we take it on?

A. Well, to be honest, you have a few questions wrapped up there – but they're all interconnected. You are positioned against a competitor who is bigger than you and is cheaper than you. So don't fight on either of those two fronts because you cannot win. Even if you decided that a good marketing strategy was to reduce your prices, your competitor would probably be able to react and do the same, but reduce their prices for longer. You've got to get back to basics. Sell! Sell your differentiators which are – I presume – your smaller size and hence your agility, responsiveness, better customer service… Search out the customers who are willing to buy those things and ensure your margins are proportionally higher so you can invest in customer service.

Q. How do you sell when your competitor is better than you?

A. Well, what do you mean by 'better'? Do you think they are better? There must be some reasons why your customers choose you – what are they? And whatever they are, you need to sell those more strongly. Ensure that both you and your sales team are doing everything they can to get those potential 'buying criteria' into the minds of your clients. Turn those features into advantages, and into benefits.

22. Being the best version of you

However much you study the great business leaders – the Richard Bransons or Jack Welches – you can't be them. What you can be, though, is the best version of you. How?

Here's how to get the job that allows you to be the best version of you, through a clear proactive approach.

There is a version of you which is extraordinary, amazing and would make you feel very much 'the best version of you'. A lot of the time you would feel 'in the zone'. You'd be paid for what you do but in many ways that would seem crazy because you would love your work so much!

Does that seem too ridiculous? Well, many of the people you admire in business are good at what they do because they have noticed and exploited what they are good at, rather than choosing a good career, even if that means ignoring formal education. So, how do you get to be the best version of you? One exercise, two stages and three factors. Please read on…

One exercise

Take a short break; ten to fifteen minutes would be ideal. Don't 'do' anything during that time. Just walk or rest and let your mind wander; don't read on until your time is up. Then grab some paper and a pen and answer the following questions as quickly as you can. In the working context:

- What do you love?
- What do you hate?
- When do you feel at your best?
- When does time, well, become timeless?
- Is there any work which you love so much that you would do it for free?

Now take another short break and come back and review your answers. You may well find that this gives you some insight into the best version of you.

Here's an idea for you...

Be proactive with the job you want; don't wait for the job advertisement which is looking for you. Try and create the role of your dreams where you are, or contact organisations who have such a role. Write, ring and propose. If you are truly passionate about that role it will come across and the role will be yours. Don't expect instant success; keep trying and be willing to take intermediate positions to help you build experience.

Two stages

- The 'do it' stage. Do your utmost to pursue that career, that passion. This may simply need you to have a discussion with your boss, or it might be a three-year quest, but it'll be worth it. To keep you inspired and focused and motivated on this quest, start reading the biographies of those you admire. You'll notice this 'on a quest' point as a constant in their lives rather than the reluctant 'I've got to get a job'!
- The 'learn' stage. Continue to amplify what you enjoy and look for opportunities to leave out what you do not, in your current career and in any new career you take up. If you start a business, continue to 'morph' it so that it allows you to play to your strengths rather than suffering your weaker points. One particularly interesting variation on this is the portfolio career, in which

91

you have a collection of mini-careers all running at the same time, maybe a part-time job with an IT company for two days a week or your own low-key, often evening, consultancy. Then you also sell your artwork online.

Three factors

- The 'don't be worried about what others think' factor. There are many 'prescribed' routes for you in your career, life and culture; these will not necessarily allow you to express yourself. Sure, it would be prestigious to be marketing director within a brand-recognised organisation, but is it really you? Would it get you out of bed in the morning with a leap and a bound? Yes? Great! No? Maybe consider something else.
- The 'you'll change' factor. As you grow and develop – and doing the job 'which you are destined to do' should particularly allow this kind of development – you will change your desires over time. You thought you wanted the management route, but you've discovered that it's not really you.
- The 'you'll know' factor. This is the answer to the question 'how will I know whether this is it?' You'll know. Be logical, but be sensitive to your intuition and feeling; they will tell you.

It can, at times, be frightening to be making these kinds of choices and it will not be easy. In particular it might appear that you have chosen a high-risk route, but in fact by basing your career on what you truly are good at, you have made it more sustainable in the long term.

Nurture your nature. Anon

How did it go?

Q. Don't these ideas fly in the face of much conventional thinking on self-development and training, that essentially we can be and do anything?

A. That idea still holds. If you wish to become a senior officer in the police force, you probably can. Start your own consultancy? That, too. Run a coffee shop? True, also. However, unless really, truly, deep down it's what you want to do, then it is not really sustainable. The constant process of nurturing your nature will take you on to that enjoyable and sustainable path.

Q. What about various tools such as the Myers–Briggs Type Indicator and Strengthfinder which purport to tell you your strengths and hence guide you to your 'perfect' career?

A. Any recognised tools such as the two above can certainly be used to help decision making, but there is no reason to treat them as anything more than a guide. They are not 'correct' or 'absolute' and, if treated too literally, might be misleading. If answering a set of questions and getting a score could tell you your chosen career, life might be a lot simpler. There is no doubt that they can support your thinking process, though, and often offer some powerful insights. In the end it's your decision, and your feeling and intuition will guide you.

23. Act as if you are the CEO

Don't wait for permission: do it – and 99% of the time you will get away with it. The other 1% of the time you can always apologise!

And when they need a new CEO, guess who will be the natural choice?

Of course, it doesn't need to be the CEO; whatever job or career you are after in the business world, 'act as if'. Act as if you had it. Act as a manager would. Act as a senior consultant would. Then you'll be a natural choice when the formal selection comes along. A quick word of warning here; I'm not talking about stepping beyond your expertise or advising without knowledge. But I am talking about developing the gravitas a director might possess or the listening skills of someone who is at a senior level. And more. Time to get going on structuring your thinking – read on…

Develop the CEO (or sales director or team leader or…) mindset

- Do it, and apologise if necessary rather than not do it at all. Say a client is in danger of being lost if something is not done and done quickly, but nobody is willing to make a decision. All those who officially can do so are out, so you OK the refund. That's CEO thinking.

■ No failure, only feedback. Here's an example: you collate some data and ask to make a five-minute pitch to the board on how flexitime would boost, not lower, productivity. More CEO thinking.

■ 'I can.' Think positively. You can get to grips with numbers – yes, you can! Again, that's CEO thinking.

Develop CEO working practices

■ Have a personal vision. Where do you want to be in five years' time?

■ Have timed plans: a year plan, a quarter plan, a month plan, a week plan, and a day plan. Start 'helicopter view' and 'come into land' – look them up online if you don't know what they are.

■ Do what is necessary, such as setting an objective for a meeting.

■ Do the things others cannot be bothered to do. Always turning up on time is a good one.

■ Do the small things which make the difference, such as thanking people, even for 'just doing their job'.

Create a support team

Who can help you be even better than you are now? Your support team, of course. Ah – you don't have one? Start building a collection of like-minded individuals who help each other. They help you; you help them. Aim for at least a strategic thinker, a pragmatist, a lateral thinker, a financial wizard and a relationships guru.

Here's an idea for you...

Write a 500-word story called 'A Day in the Life of [the perfect role you seek]'. Here's an example: 'As newly promoted HR Manager I call the team together and announce that there will be no immediate changes, but that I will be talking to each of them separately about what changes they might like to see which would make a more effective team. I would also ask them what is one thing they would like me to do to make their relationship with me easier...' Then review the story and ask yourself 'Even though I am not HR manager [or whatever] yet, what could I do?'

Dress for success

You know it makes a difference…

For men, these things can help and are often given insufficient attention.

- Great hygiene, especially hair and particularly if long.
- Think very carefully about designer stubble. If you're in the media, perhaps; everybody else, get a close shave!
- Suit and tie. Certainly have a jacket available: it will distinguish you. If you're not a natural with dress sense at least find out which is your better colour, grey or blue. Then get an interesting tie, but not a ridiculous one or something covered in cartoon characters.
- Polished shoes.
- If it's casual, then clean chinos, a polo shirt, V-neck jumper and/or blazer can work well.

While these can hinder:

- T-shirts. They're only OK in the right places, such as young / technical / non-customer-facing environments.
- Torn jeans. Never.
- Tired suits. Never.
- Oily ties. Never.

For women, these can help:

- Keep it simple: clean lines and no fuss.
- Zero or minimal jewellery.
- If you don't know, get advice on what colour/s work for you.

While these can hinder:

■ Too short a skirt

■ Too revealing a top

■ Too tight an outfit

■ Too low a trouser band

Finally, try and get some variation on the 'easy' black city suit worn almost everywhere, every day in some environments; add a splash of colour.

Remember that your appearance is not just your clothes; the following can also reveal a lot about you:

■ Your pen

■ Your notebook

■ Your briefcase or bag

Acting is the least mysterious of all crafts. Whenever we want something from somebody or when we want to hide something or pretend, we're acting. Most people do it all day long. Marlon Brando

How did it go?

Q. *Sorry to put a dampener on your enthusiasm. Isn't this 'acting' all a little high risk?*

A. It certainly shouldn't be: the key point is that you are 'acting as if…' with your soft skills, not your technical and advisory skills, so there is no danger of you going beyond your 'official' remit. What you are doing is subtly adding more power to the equation of you equals your technical/functional capability multiplied by your interpersonal skills. It's the latter that you are improving, to a significant degree.

Q. *I'd love to do this but I am a little concerned about cynicism from my colleagues. How do I deal with it?*

A. Cynicism now or later? When you are on your way to the top, you'll get a lot of cynicism. Start tackling it now, and then it'll be like the proverbial water off a duck's back later. Don't judge others, but certainly don't react to their comments. Your success is simply reminding them of what they could be doing – but aren't!

24. Keep a notebook. Make decisions. Act

Most MBA lecture notes go into folders, never to be looked at again. Many reading lists are never acted upon. So many case studies are, well, not used as case studies.

Not you, though. Invest in that notebook; keep it with you at all times, capture essential wisdom and act. Start turning decisions into actions.

It can be intensely frustrating, this study process: the more you study, the less you actually learn. Huh? Well, the new folder starts out empty; then the first set of lecture notes is added, plus the handouts, the case studies and the URL references. You dutifully read them, then there is another lecture to go to, a project team meeting to attend – and suddenly, at best, you're sitting in lectures and acting as a file clerk. And not actually using or implementing any of the valuable new ideas. No, you have made the wise decision to manage your own MBA which means you have a high likelihood that your studies will be turned into action – and that's presumably why you are doing them. Here's how to make studying your own MBA highly effective.

Here's an idea for you...

As you read any book or article for your MBA studies, take a few notes. Those notes are likely to be decisions and may be reflections: things you are considering, things you want to do. Take each decision and turn it into an action. For it to be an action it needs to have two components at least – to be measurable and to have a time limit. Here's a quick example for you. Jot down in your notebook, 'run an off-site meeting to identify pricing policy'. Turn that into fixing the date for the meeting by Friday, and circulate the briefing document by Friday week. Decisions turned into actions are immensely empowering.

- Minimise input. The less you read and digest, the more likely you are to be able to do something with the ideas. However, that does not mean do not read broadly, it does not mean do not gain depth; it simply means choose your texts. Take any reading list and reduce it. Take the four titles on competitiveness by an author and reduce it to two books. Read less, act more.

- Have clear, visible objectives for your studies. Why are you doing this studying thing? Interest? To become a consultant or a better consultant? To improve your business? As a precursor to a 'real' MBA? It focuses your mind, doesn't it? Write down why you are doing this work on your own MBA and keep that statement clear and visible. It'll stop you from getting distracted.

- Look for application and reality. When you are reading, bear in mind your objectives; you are probably seeking lots of 'how to' information. So concentrate on real and practical and relevant material. Skip and avoid the theoretical, the obtuse, the too abstract or background material that you can do without.

- Make your notes 'road-worthy'. It's very easy to be so busy scribbling and/or typing to forget that one day you might actually want to use this idea you are capturing. So as you write or type, do so for later reference. If there is nothing else that you do to produce decent notes, always put a reference at the bottom as to your source. That's not there for your tutor or your examiner – it's to help you!

- Ask provocative questions such as who, what, why should I believe that and is there more evidence? Curiosity helps learning. Be as provocative as you can! How could Porter have drawn that conclusion? Did Belbin do any other research? Would that work in Europe? What about now as opposed to a decade ago?
- Immediate use. Once you come across an idea, try and use it immediately; that will wire in the skills.

Finally, focus on some process skills. Invest a bit of your time in learning how to learn; the return is good. Here are three ideas which are highly likely to be worth the investment, in order of increasing complexity:

- Page layout. If you are taking notes by hand, consider pre-ruling each page and creating some sections. You might rule the page into two-thirds and one-third sections, and then use the latter section for 'pulling out' actions.
- SQ3R by Harry Maddox. Maddox researched and created a simple but powerful study technique: S is survey the materials, then Q for ask questions to guide your learning, then the three Rs – read the material, recite it back and, then, finally revise. A great little tool.
- Mind-mapping by Tony Buzan. Buzan is strongly associated with a technique known as mind-mapping and although several authors have created variants, his has the advantage of plenty of source materials. Mind-mapping allows the capture of large amounts of information in a highly visual way and in a compressed format.

A decision is not a decision until you have taken an action. Anthony Robbins

How did it go?

Q. Surely not all notes, reflections and jottings are actual actions or need to become so?

A. True to a certain extent. If you have the luxury of pure academic study then much reading is there 'in the background' where your brain will work on the matter, perhaps only synthesising something years later. However, most people in the business world need to be more pragmatic and are looking for an immediate return. Hence do try and turn any jotting into an action.

Q. What is the structure for a good action?

A. The famous and useful acronym is SMART – make sure the action is specific and measurable, achievable, realistic and timely. It's not just a neat acronym; it works!

25. Successful consultancy

One of the reasons you may be doing an MBA is to become a consultant, maybe internal, maybe external. Here's how to start a consultancy which is high-end and successful.

Follow the guidance and you can make it happen: five stages to success.

It doesn't really matter whether it's your own business, or whether it's a department within an organisation. Now, for ease of description, I'll assume you are starting your own external consultancy. But remember the same thinking essentially applies if you are attempting to turn your HR department into an internal HR consultancy – exactly the same thinking. You should feel confident that you can answer the question 'If we were to outsource, would we survive?' with a very positive 'Yes!'

Stage 1: what's its purpose?
Today is the day to get clear. Why do you want to start your own business and, in particular, why do you want to start a consultancy? Be honest: is it for the money? That's fine, of course. To change the world? To have more free time? You need to

Here's an idea for you...

You may not like it, but you know
that programme *Dragons' Den*?
Present your idea to an imaginary
Dragons' Den. How would you
fare? Think about the no-nonsense
grilling you would get from the
panel; they are not easily
impressed. They've seen it all
before and would go beyond your
naive enthusiasm; they'd ridicule
and bully you. Is that mean? A
little, but it's probably better to go
through this now rather than later,
having lost your house and
acquired a string of debts.

be clear, though – how much money? Change the world in
what way? How much free time and for what purpose? Get
clear; get explicit. Now, ask yourself again why you really
want to do it.

Now answer this question: how will you position it as a
premium consultancy? What will be special about it? Are
you now clear on your purpose? Successful entrepreneurs
tend to have purpose and they tend to have clarity of
purpose. Now document and/or draw your purpose and
put it somewhere you will see it every day, both now while
you are planning and eventually while you are running the
business. If you are running an internal consultancy, these
questions are just as crucial.

Stage 2: why is it different?

To do more than just survive, to make money and to have a
comfortable lifestyle, you must be distinct. The bottom line is be distinct or be
extinct. So, why would anyone want to buy from you? The answer (I hope) is not
because you offer the lowest prices; no, you have something special. But here's
the irony: if you do have anything special – whether that's a widget or a
methodology – it won't stay special for very long. So, your secret weapon is to be
distinct on your service and responsiveness. Do not ignore that aspect. You must
have something which is unique about you; if not, you will just be selling on
price. Start work now on what your unique selling propositions are.

Stage 3: what's the plan?

In particular, have you done your gap analysis? You need a plan to take you from where you are now to where you want to be. Try answering these questions: Why would anyone buy your product? What problem are you solving? What is the price for your services? (That seems expensive! How do you justify that?) Do you know how to create an invoice or chase for payment? Could you confidently do a pitch for new business? What is your marketing budget? What will you use it for? Can you manage a cash flow or motivate a team? Document your plan – now.

Stage 4: getting better all the time!

Your business is up and running; you've got customers and clients. What do they like about you? What do they love about you? What really annoys them? Document and improve, constantly and continuously. Get better all the time.

Stage 5: success is a journey.

You're on the way, but you are actually never there. Regularly take time out to review the above questions and reinvent your business. Remember that your biggest blocker to long-term success is, ironically, your current success.

Pointy-haired boss: 'We can't compete on price. We also can't compete on quality, features or service. That leaves fraud, which I'd like you to call marketing.'

Scott Adams, *Dilbert*

How did it go?

Q. This is proving really difficult and I have talked to loads of people, searched the Internet a lot and read a fair few books… what on earth do I charge for my services?

A. Mmm. You're right: it's a tricky one. Too high a price and you never get a chance to show how good you are. Too low and not only are you immediately losing money but it's difficult to raise your prices later. So here are some practical ideas. Firstly, there is no correct price; offer excellent value and charge for it. Secondly, consider your competitors: what do they charge? Consider charging more than them as you are going to be better than them, aren't you? Finally, regularly review and increase your prices as your reputation increases.

Q. I've got bogged down in getting business, obviously new business, but also hanging on to current business. How do I go about it?

A. Word of mouth. Word of mouth. Word of mouth. If you are an internal consultancy, you want your customers to say you are wonderful. If you're an external consultancy, they also should say you are wonderful. Nothing compares to it. Your goal is to help accelerate word of mouth by doing a fantastic job, asking for references, asking for introductions and sorting out problems. That's it; do all of those and you will be inundated with quality work.

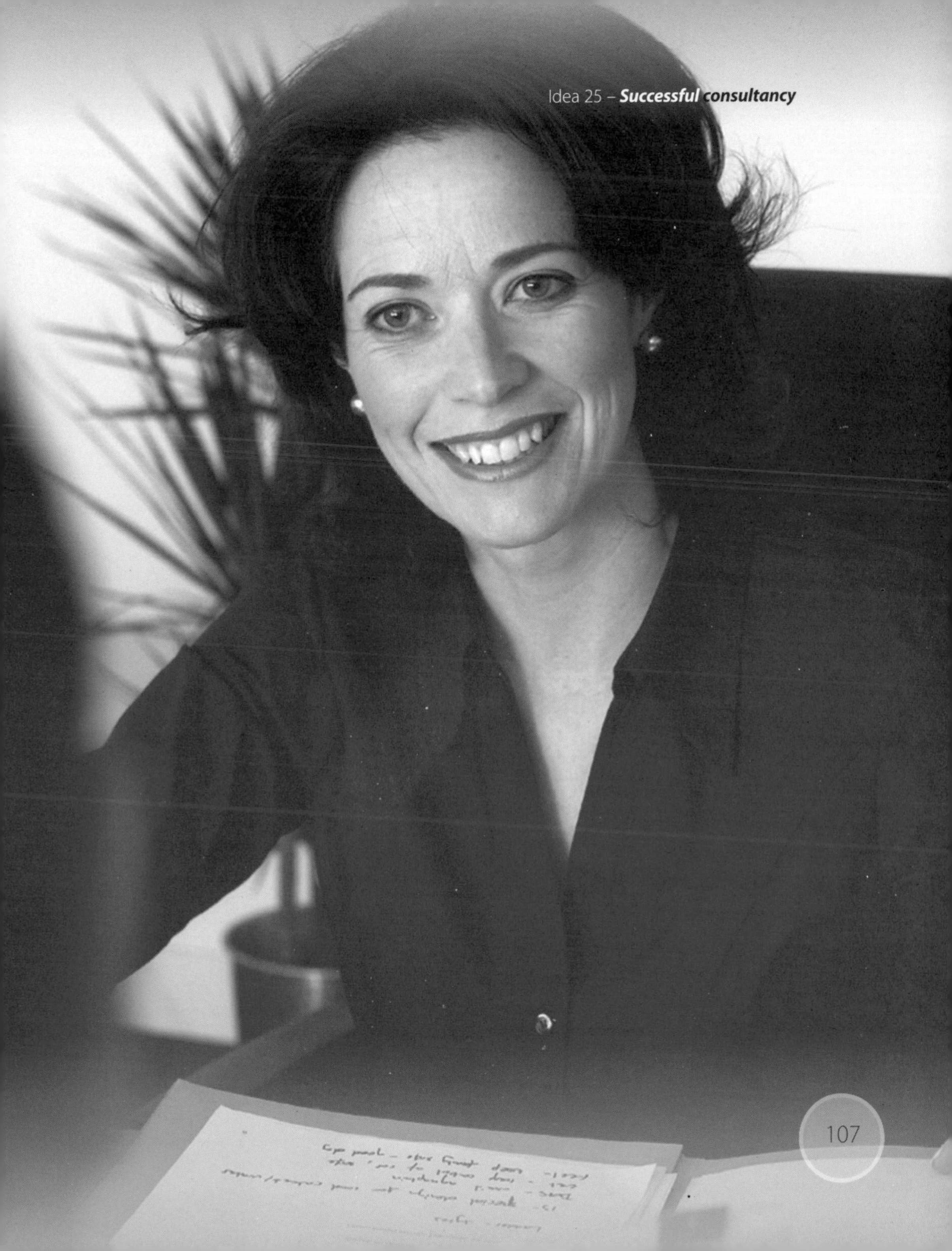

26. Financial feedback

How to read those statements.

And I can make it soooo easy, too!

A critical MBA skill is clearly the ability to attempt to assess the financial health of an organisation. There are three major documents to consider:

- The balance sheet. This is a 'point in time' picture of the health of the company concerned.
- The profit and loss account. This illustrates whether an organisation is making money and making profit.
- The cash-flow statement. This identifies where the cash is, and cash clearly is different to profit.

I'll expand on each of the above terms fully in a moment, but…

- Firstly, most MBA students will not get much further than being competent amateurs with accounting – unless, of course, that is their chosen profession. And many scandals over the past few years have reminded everyone of how easy it is to hide the financial truth from apparent public scrutiny.
- Secondly, financial viability tends to be a snapshot and cannot really be anything else. You have to put this in the context of whether there will be future growth, of whether the business or the market is in decline.
- Thirdly, the culture of the organisation and its management team has to be taken into consideration as well.

The overall viability of an organisation is a complex mix which is not just the financial factors. Now that I've stated that, let's go back to the basics on the figures.

The balance sheet

To realise the power of the balance sheet, it may help to begin as follows. If somebody earns a high salary, are they wealthy? Well, not necessarily, of course. If you wanted to know whether somebody was wealthy it would be immaterial whether they earned 10K or 50K or 300K a year. You'd want to know what they owned – or, more formally, their personal balance sheet. You'd do that, of course, by taking their assets (e.g. cash, a house, a car), subtracting their liabilities (such as their mortgage or any other debts). The difference would be their worth or, more strictly, their personal net worth. If you did that with a small business, assets might include ideas, and the difference between the two – i.e. assets and liabilities – is what is known as the equity.

Right, that's not so difficult. I need to step up the jargon for the next stage, though. In a large business you do the same process but assets could now be something like plant and equipment and liabilities could be tax liabilities. The difference between the two is generally referred to as the shareholder value. Hence the famous equation: assets equals liabilities plus share capital. To be honest if you can get your head around all that, unless you are becoming a specialist, that's great.

Here's an idea for you...

Step 1: add up your assets (cash, house, etc.). Step 2: add up your liabilities (mortgage, loans, etc.). Take the latter from the former. What's the answer? Positive is great. Negative – well, not so bad, especially if it's a well-managed mortgage. If it is negative you almost certainly want to get it positive as soon as you can. Notice the power that information gives you. You've got a great understanding of what a balance sheet is and you also get to understand your personal wealth which will put you in a good position for the next stage of your career. That's exactly what it does for businesses, as long as the business can understand it – and that's where you can help.

Profit and loss account

The profit and loss account is very important because business is about money and the only money which is really of interest is profit. The profit and loss account will tell you for a chosen time period – like a month or a quarter or a year – what the sales have been, what the costs have been and hence give you the profit for that period.

Which brings me to the cash flow...

We may all be in the business of profit, but even profitable companies can be brought down without cash – hence the saying that 'cash is king'. The cash-flow statement shows whether cash is coming in or out and the goal is always to have positive cash flow. This may be achieved by careful cash management or the choice of business to ensure positive cash flow.

Money / It's a crime / Share it fairly / But don't take a slice of my pie. / Money / So they say / Is the root of all evil today.

Pink Floyd, from *The Dark Side of the Moon*

How did it go?

Q. I just can't get excited about this boring stuff. Marketing, yes; people, yes. But numbers… is it just me?

A. No, it's not just you; it's very common and many people really flunk the finance part of their MBA. But it is useful. For example, you don't want to become a great strategic marketer who can't 'talk the numbers', nor do you want to be an HR specialist who really doesn't understand the full implications of head-count costs, so I encourage you to work at it. The breakthrough often comes when you make it personal, so do it for your own house, do it for your own business or do it for your own client. Make it personal, then it is relevant and then you will understand it.

Q. We work increasingly in international markets. Are these statements the same the world over?

A. Basically, yes. Clearly you will want to employ local experts, if necessary, especially when concerned with tax and local practice. But essentially the core ideas are the same the world over. Good news!

27. New World of Work drivers 2: automation

Time for another look at what lies behind the management and leadership which is needed in the New World of Work. Now, it's the impact of technology...

Yes, it's about how the world of work will be converted into a room full of humming silicon chips. Bad news for some, but not for you...

Putting it in context

The term 'the New World of Work' is a convenient title for the world of work as it is now. This somewhat different world came into existence about ten years ago – when the use of email became commonplace – and is quite different to the Old World of Work. There are seven drivers of change which have caused a significant change in the way we work – from Old World of Work to New World of Work – and one is undoubtedly automation. Of course, automation has been happening for hundreds of years; I'm simply concerned here with the increasing penetration of automation throughout the workplace. This, together with the current and rapidly increasing rate of change, has had an effect on some practical physiological parameters (such as thinking speed, for instance).

Automation

In the New World of Work, technology allows us to replace many normal human interactions – a conversation, a face-to-face meeting, a memo – with something which is faster but stripped of real human emotion or feeling; email being the most ubiquitous example. And why is this a problem? Because human beings need touch, they need contact, they are not objects or machines, nor are they 'resources'. And herein lies a major problem. Things you would never say to someone's face, or even on the phone for that matter, become all too easy to mistakenly say through an email. The relentless efficiency of automation often causes the sheer level of workload to be so high that it removes from individuals their ability to be effective. Some of the worst of (often male) aggressive behaviours become encouraged; some of the best of (generally female) discursive behaviours often get eliminated. The organisation loses its soul. And that is not a healthy organisation to be in or to be involved with.

Implications for organisations

An organisation without soul or spirit or life or positive culture – whatever you like to call it – is unlikely to be a place where people give of their best. What can be done? Well, there is a three-part strategy of which you may well need to become a champion:

- Articulate the problem. Everyone knows that email can be very bad for constructive relationships, and we all know that too much efficiency is not at

Here's an idea for you...

Think about your business or, if you prefer, one of your clients. Consider some problem area such as poor teamwork or miscommunication between departments. Got an example? It won't be hard to find something, unfortunately. What do you think is the real root of the problem? I know that you'll be most likely to say something like 'rubbish communication' and I would agree, but what causes it to be so bad? Perhaps too much of it is dependent on technology – check it out; I'm sure you'll find that it's obvious. So how could you remedy the situation?

all effective. The same is true of the fact that speed of work is not a replacement for quality of thinking. So recognise it.

■ Then decide to address the issue. Encourage people to think about what kind of communication is really needed, hard or soft. Hard communication is the giving of simple data; there is little that can be misunderstood or debated, and email is a good means for that. But there is also soft communication, and it's equally vital. That's about feelings, morale and more complicated issues, and it requires face-to-face communication.

■ Reward what is known as 'high-touch' leadership. Yes, still reward those people who succeed and who hit their goals, but in particular reward leaders who work for the long term, who work at relationships, who connect with other people in a high-touch way.

Implications for you

As with organisations, the first step is to recognise the problem, both in the way you might deal with others and in the way you are dealt with. Then you need to address the issue; the simplest way to do this is to make sure you communicate as much as you can in a high-touch rather than in a high-tech way. Finally, choose to work as much as possible in a high-touch environment.

Bit by bit the logic of the network will overtake every atom we deal with.

Kevin Kelly, founding executive editor of *Wired* magazine

How did it go?

Q. *So how do I ensure that I am not replaced by a silicon chip?*

A. Well, by assuming (and hoping?) that it will be a very long time before the silicon chip can replace human emotions such as empathy and inspiration, to name just two highly complex but highly valuable human abilities. Empathy, for example, is central to great customer service, as is inspiration to outstanding leadership. So try to develop your own abilities in those areas to recognisably excellent levels. You could also ensure your survival by choosing a career where such human abilities are required and valued.

Q. *But is there really time in the New World of Work to be high touch?*

A. It sometimes appears not, but that's an illusion. Of course the quick email gets the job 'sorted', passes the issue on. But does it fully explain it? Does it truly resolve it? Possibly. Possibly not. And if the issue has not been fully explained and/or resolved then it has not been handled truly effectively and will unravel at some later stage. That, of course, only creates more time-management issues. No, true productivity is definitely about being high touch. Sure, it needs time; but that time is paid back many times later.

28. Get a personal development plan

If there is one thing you must leave this MBA with, it's a personal development plan: how will you stay employable for the next decade? One heck of a question...

I'll help you get some great and exciting answers.

One strong theme – as you are very well aware – on your personal MBA quest is to maximise your employability, to reduce your vulnerability and to safeguard your choice over the career you seek. But in a world which is increasingly one market with a few dominant players, that is becoming tougher and tougher to do. Guess what – you need a plan.

You need a personal development plan, to be specific. Now, if you are currently employed, especially with a large employer, my guess is that you already have one of these. But my guess also is that it is fairly short and focused on making you of more use to your employer (naturally!). It will have plenty of discussion about competencies and the need to do this, that and the other. All well and good. I want to help you get a plan together which is about you and your career – with or without your current employer. Of course, if you are currently between jobs or if you run your own business then you are very unlikely to have a plan, and yet you need one most of all.

To help, here are the components of this plan:
■ Step 1: Where am I now?
   This defines your current job and role.

Example: I am product marketing manager at
LowerThanYours Jeans
Tip: Write down a few of the responsibilities for the job;
that will help you with the next question.

- Step 2: Where do I want to be in three years?
It's now time to start doing some serious thinking. You
may well need to take a break and come back to this. But
this is classic consultancy practice – you need to know
where you are going to; what is the change you seek?
Example: I want to be a marketing director in the leisure
industry. I believe the leisure industry will continue to
grow and become more important whereas pure retail
will stay volatile.
Tip: Define this as fully as you can.

- Step 3: What exactly is the gap?
Define this in every way possible. Skills, thinking, geography…
Example: At the moment I certainly have no idea how a director is meant to
operate and my CV would not look at all attractive for the position. I need to up
my skills, I need to up my experience. Courses will help but I am planning to run
a consultancy alongside my main job to get some sharp-end experience…
Tip: Write plenty on this.

- Step 4: What do I need to close the gap?
Example: I'm going to get on my company's leadership course, pay for myself
to go on some Institute of Directors' courses and start my own business. Then
I'll review this plan in nine months' time.
Tip: Be specific.

Here's an idea for you...

If you could do your dream job, what
would it be? Go off and think about
it. No 'ifs and buts'. Get the dream
first and make it sensory rich. What
would it look like? (Definitely in a
major city, maybe San Francisco…)
What would it smell like? (Those
Singapore markets…) What would
you hear? (The buzz and chatter of a
great marketing team, the accolade
of another award-winning
campaign…) Write it up, maybe
draw it up. Create something strong
in words and perhaps strong visually
and put it somewhere where you
will see it every day.

- Step 5: What are ten actions I need to take over the coming months to initiate those actions?
  Example: 1. See HR to get on the leadership course. 2. Ask to see my manager re more responsibility…
  Tip: Create ten definite actions – that will force you to get very specific.

- Step 6: What might block me?
  Consider anything that might get in the way of your plans.
  Example: Time. My manager is currently very distracted about her own career and not much interested in mine.
  Tip: Detail each blocker and break them down.

- Step 7: How can I overcome or pre-empt those blockers?
  Here you need to identify the solution for each individual blocker.
  Example: To overcome the time problem, I need to schedule some fixed time on a regular basis to work on my own plans.
  Tip: Most blockers tend to come down to time. Recognise that you won't have time, so what you need to do is make time.

- Step 8: Plan, review and improve. Make a diary note to improve the plan on a monthly or even weekly basis. Create a 'recurring event' in your electronic schedule.

Life is like riding a bicycle. To keep your balance you must keep moving. Albert Einstein

How did it go?

Q. *How detailed should the plan be?*

A. The most important aspects of your plan are the actions. These actions should be SMART: specific, measurable, achievable, realistic and time-bound with the two most critical being measurable and time-bound. To make it clear, here's an objective that is not remotely SMART: 'work on my directorship skills'. This one, however, is: 'learn all the necessary legal rulings for a director according to the Institute of Directors' website by September of this year.'

Q. *I am already thinking of changing my plan. Does that mean it was a rubbish plan?*

A. No. Your ideas will change and, just as with any company strategy, you will tend to only get clarity about what you really want to do as you start doing it. If your plan is changing it is probably becoming stronger; the most important thing is to keep it up to date. It shouldn't cause you to feel restricted in your thinking. On the other hand, if you don't commit to some actions in the end it's unlikely you'll get the changes you seek. It really is a careful balance.

29. Numbers!

You've been avoiding them, haven't you? Those terms such as liquidity make you feel a little edgy! And those ratios?

Well: numbers are power, numbers help you win your case. Let's get good with numbers, quickly and easily.

The background

Economics is the science that studies the production, distribution and consumption of goods and services. Adam Smith was a key player in the development of modern economics when he wrote an amazing book called *The Wealth of Nations*. In this he put a strong case for the support of free markets, and argued that they would ultimately regulate themselves.

Then there are economic cycles. Here two useful terms are:
- Inflation. This is the pressure on prices to go up, the consequence being that you get less for your money.
- Recession. The economy does not grow for two consecutive quarters.

Now for economic health. Five useful 'big picture' measures are:
- GDP or Gross Domestic Product. The total value of (new) goods and services produced in the UK.
- GNP or Gross National Product. This is GDP plus used goods.
- RPI or Retail Price Index. The change in price of a specified basket of goods. Every so often the basket of goods is updated (which can be a fascinating insight into

our changing buying habits, in itself). RPI is a useful inflation indicator.

- Unemployment. The number of people out of work; a high figure naturally leads to concern.
- Balance of Trade. Take exports and subtract imports. It's best if this is positive, of course.

Now for more detail...

- Forecast. This is an attempt to predict how much money will be generated, often by particular parts of a business, say by the sales department. It is worth putting significant time and attention into developing the correct competence at forecasting; it's a careful blend of process (such as tracking market conditions) and human skill (like asking probing questions of the sales team).
- Budget. An attempt to decide how much money will be needed, perhaps by a department. Problems in this area include 'sand-bagging', when experienced managers are aware that their budget is likely to be cut, anticipate this and do some deliberate padding. Again, asking rigorous questions can normally avoid such challenges.

Ratios can give you instant guidance, so let's look at them in detail.

Liquidity ratios are about solvency or the ability to generate cash.
- Current. Can you pay your current liabilities out of your current assets? A figure of two or more is considered satisfactory.
- Quick/acid. This ratio deducts stock from assets, making it an even tougher test. A figure of more than one is considered acceptable.

Here's an idea for you...

Go beyond the figures when reading annual reports. Here are some areas to be concerned about. Firstly, lack of ownership of problems. If a company is doing poorly, it must own the problems and detail action for recovery. Blaming 'bad trading conditions' demonstrates a lack of leadership. Then look for a lack of planning and/or precision in that planning. Yes, the company wants growth, to gain market share – but how? Then consider an over-focus on reward for senior people. Line after line of big bonuses in tough trading conditions – and weak performance – is a deeply concerning sign.

Activity ratios:

- Receivables. This is, essentially, how quickly your customers pay their bills. The higher the number, the better it is.
- Average collecting period. In this case, the lower the number, the better. Work hard to get this number down and set up simple and effective money-chasing procedures.
- Stock turnover. How quickly is stock sold and replaced? Clearly you want a high turnover of stock.

Debt ratios:

- Debt to equity. Too much debt can be dangerous and this ratio measures exposure to outside creditors. A figure which is greater than one is considered worrying.

Profitability ratios:

- Profit. Profit per unit of revenue; the higher the better.
- Gross margin. This is gross profit less the cost of goods.
- RoI (Return on Investment). A magic number that shows how good you are at creating profit. The amount of money generated per unit of revenue invested.

The age of chivalry is gone. — That of sophisters, economists and calculators has succeeded; and the glory of Europe is extinguished for ever.

Edmund Burke, 18th century British politician

How did it go?

Q. One of the reasons I am doing this MBA work is that I plan to start my own business. I'll be honest, I hate every aspect of this numbers thing. My business will be selling hand-knitted, bespoke, upmarket cardigans, so do I really need to get competent at the figures?

A. No, but I would strongly encourage you to have a broad understanding, essentially as I have detailed here. Then find an excellent bookkeeper and accountant – excellent in that they are competent but also in that you can trust them. Then ask for regular reports and keep all your tax and revenue payments up to date. You'll be fine. Don't worry!

Q. Can you tell me the very essence of all this financial stuff?

A. Yes. You need to know why you are in business. It's highly likely that part of it is to make money – even if money isn't really of interest to you as such, but you need money to fund, say, your gallery. Once you know you need money you must realise that not all money is the same; you particularly want profit. Finally, once you are getting profit it's nice to make more of it, because then you can do more of what you want to do. And that's it!

30. Find, motivate and keep!

That's the HR function at its best: recruiting excellent people, helping you get the best out of them and then ensuring you don't lose them too soon.

Let's find out how it's done.

Whatever great strategies an organisation has, whatever wonderful products are in the pipeline, in the end it all comes down to the people who are in that business. Great organisations have great people. They might join 'great' and become 'outstanding' or join 'pretty good' and become 'great'. But your organisation needs to be full of great people if it is going to survive and thrive in the New World of Work. So, what's to be done?

Find the best

This is clearly the first stage; the better the people coming into the organisation, the easier for everyone. You can train and you can develop and you can motivate. But if people are good when they arrive that means the job is easier. You can find the best in various ways.

- People find people. Ask everyone in your organisation to recommend good people for vacancies. Someone who is currently doing a job knows exactly what is needed and is therefore ideal for identifying good match recruits. 'But', you say, 'won't they just put forward all their friends, especially if there is a reward?' No, because they know that the person they suggest reflects on them. It's a good idea to have monetary rewards for this service. After all, you are saving a lot in fees, advertising and time but you are also gaining a significant lower risk of an error. Pretty priceless, really.

■ Active recruitment. Place advertisements and run a campaign; the traditional stuff we've all experienced, of course. It does work but it is very hard work and, for many organisations, the final quality of output is low. How can you increase your likelihood of success? By defining who you want before you start the campaign! One of the big frustrations for HR is discovering the brief they were given has 'morphed' over time; encourage your internal client to get clear on what they want before they start seeing candidates.

■ Indirect. Ensure that your customers and suppliers know that you are always looking for great people. Make it easy to find out what is available via your website; have links on the bottom of all advertising, emails and at exhibitions. It's easy and it's free and it will 'flush out' good people.

■ Agency. An agency can do active and indirect recruitment for you, for a fee. You'll need to recruit them first, of course. Go beyond the gloss and the smart London office; do they really understand what you are after and are you a good match for them (or are they more interested in their other clients and you are fodder for trainee account managers)?

■ Be creative. You'll meet good people. Without going mad, see if you can find a place for them in you organisation. Don't lose good people when you meet them; they are rare.

One small proviso: if a great person is not well cared for and not looked after when they arrive, they will leave. Probably quite quickly.

Here's an idea for you...

So, what's your career been to date? How many positions or roles have you had? What made you move each time? What motivates you now? Especially if you have been working for ten years or more, what motivated you when you started? And does that motivate you now, or is it something different? If you answered those questions honestly you will have realised that either you are a crazy, mixed-up kid (only teasing) or this business of finding, growing and keeping people is complicated (or both). It's complicated; decide to get good at it. It's what your business is: people.

Get the best out of the best

Any individual normally admits – and their manager normally admits, too – that they have so much more potential. You need to get it out of them. Here are some practical methods:

- Skill training. Teach and re-teach them how to do their job. If you can help with formal qualifications do that, too.
- Personal development. Train people to understand themselves, their strengths and weaknesses and what makes them tick.
- Coaching. Iron out the little bugs of weaknesses via one-to-one work.
- Feedback. People may not like it, but if done with care and sensitivity it tells them how they are doing and hence how they can dramatically improve.

Keep the best

- Catch people doing things right. Once the basics have been sorted, the biggest single motivator of someone is genuine praise. Easy really, isn't it? But so rarely done…
- Growth. The basic motivators are the essentials, often known as 'hygiene factors', such as a desk, a computer. Then there is a salary which people feel rewards them properly for their capabilities. But the real motivator is growth and appropriate challenge. That's the one which must be harnessed if you are to keep good people. Great money – although nice – will not compensate for a 'stultified soul'.

You need massive recruitment to tell the poorest of the poor what is possible.

Jonathan Kozol, writer and educator

How did it go?

Q. Should we do the recruitment ourselves or get an agency to help?

A. It doesn't really matter. The costs are more hidden if you do it; they are clear if you pay an agency. A good agency will do a great job but it can take time to find one that isn't just 'shifting bodies'. You must still invest the time in creating a clear brief; otherwise you waste both a lot of time and money.

Q. How much is the going rate for 'people find people'?

A. It varies hugely for role and industry, but it needs to be significant to get people to work at it and persevere (for example, get their friend to fill in the form online, etc.). So certainly thousands of pounds, euros or dollars rather than hundreds.

31. Tutorial 1 – how to learn

You can still have tutorials with an instant MBA! Here's your first, on that thorny topic which concerns all students: how to get to grips with the material.

Pull up a comfy chair and help yourself to a cup of tea.

However you're doing your MBA, there's plenty of 'stuff' to get to grips with: thought leaders and their concepts, classical financial literacy, the latest thinking on total quality management… the list goes on (and seems to get longer). It's the constant bane of the student. Hopefully I can help in this tutorial and give you some top tips from successful students.

Tip 1: Getting through large volumes of material

Reading is the basis of such 'wisdom' – there is no doubt about that at all. If you wish to stay up to date and to continue to build your expertise you must continue the learning process, and reading is one of the best ways. Here are a few tips to make that volume of reading easier.

- Never start a book without a good 'why?' or, more specifically, 'why am I reading this book?' The answer 'because I am meant to', is not enough. There is always a reason: to make more money, to find out how to fix your client's problem… Create a good reason, because the bigger the reason, the greater will be your enthusiasm for the book.

Here's an idea for you...

Take three non-fiction books on broadly linked (but only broadly so) subjects, such as marketing strategy, creative thinking and project management. Read a chapter in one book, then another chapter from another, then something from the third. Build up speed and start jumping from one book to another; take notes as you go. Many people have said that, far from being bewildering, the break to another book stimulates their interest in all three volumes. It also helps them build connections which support memory and critical thinking. Once you have some experience, try more books in one go and make the connections between them less and less obvious.

- Remember as you read more, you will get better. In this very visual world, many people are a little out of practice at the intense reading habit, but you can learn it.
- Take notes: that gives you focus and direction, and helps understanding and memory build as you progress though the book.
- You don't have to read everything about a subject, generally, or everything by a single author. You will soon discover which the 'pivotal' books are; concentrate on those. Most thought leaders have a couple of key messages they evangelise, and these are typically encapsulated in one or two works. The rest are refinements, however valid they might be.

Tip 2: Speed reading

There seems no doubt that various approaches will help you assimilate more, and do so more quickly. However, it has to be said that some of the specialist methods can incur a big overhead in learning them. By all means research the various methodologies but do remember some that require 'trance states' – although apparently proven – also often require an expensive week-long course. Calculate the return on your investment. It is possible to get significant improvements in reading speed more simply by:

- Reading deliberately. Let go of your newspaper and/or novel-reading style and read with focus.

■ Taking notes.

■ Taking regular breaks.

■ Reading in good light and with a good posture.

Tip 3: Keeping up with the latest ideas

It can seem difficult, but the following might help. As you read and develop your MBA mind, you will become aware of certain authors and journalists who tend to be 'future-minded'. Regularly look them up online; that way you can track their thinking and see what they are noting and writing about. This will lead you to some blogs. Most of the authors you are interested in will have a blog for their initial output and thinking. Journalists, too. Be willing to comment on those blogs and/or email the writers; most like to have their ideas tested and challenged. For this to work for you, don't simply ask them for help; suggest ideas to them. Finally, try encapsulating the essential ideas and presenting them to your team – get them to challenge the ideas, too.

Thanks — you taught me how to think

An anonymous Oxford student experiencing the tutorial system, quoted by David Palfreyman in his white paper of May 2002

How did it go?

Q. I'm sold on this reading business, and I wasn't. I've really got into it; it's clearly an easy and cheap way into fresh thinking. But how on earth do I get my people to do it?

A. Let them see that you read a lot and that you use the ideas you have read about. Create a simple library of business books, available to all; encourage the reading of useful paragraphs at team meetings. Introduce the vocabulary from various books – things like the tipping point – and encourage people to discover the background to such books. It's also worth considering a reading budget of one book a month on expenses for certain people.

Q. I am so lacking in reading time at the moment. Is listening to audio books a suitable alternative?

A. Ideas from any source are good and audio versions – especially of recognised books – are particularly good. But (you knew there would be one, didn't you?), there is something very particular about reading which is extremely beneficial to developing thinking. Reading allows you to work at exactly your own rate, it allows you to stop and pause and allows you to take notes (most people listen to something like an audiobook CD in the car). These might seem trivial points but they all add up to a more powerful learning and reflective experience which in turn makes you better at application, and hence better at business.

32. New World of Work drivers 3: alternative shores

Here's the third detailed look at what lies behind management and leadership in the New World of Work. Offshoring, outsourcing: call it what you will.

Bad news for some, but not you. Here's how not to become a commodity but a specialist who is in demand — and who commands a great salary.

The context

The term 'the New World of Work' is one which is given to the world of work – now. This world came into existence perhaps ten years ago and there are seven drivers of change which have caused a significant change in the way we work; alternative shoring is the third. In one sense 'alternative shoring' has been around for a while, but there's no doubt that, with the increasing ease of and shift towards 'offshoring', it has increased. Here I'm simply concerned with the increasing ease of taking advantage of lower costs elsewhere on the planet and the global 'one market'.

Alternative shores

There is always somewhere cheaper than where you are at the moment to build things and/or from where to offer services. Callers were initially frustrated when banks set up UK call centres rather than connecting them to their branch but they got used to it – and it was a sign of much to come. As technology and the 'one market' has grown it has become increasingly viable to base products and services in different (invariably lower cost, of course) countries.

Here's an idea for you...

You need an A4 piece of paper. Rule a line down the middle vertically. Head the left-hand column with SAME and the right with DIFFERENT. Now write about yourself, assigning your assets to one of the columns. So in SAME you might put 'same degree and vocational qualifications as rest of team'; in DIFFERENT you might have 'highly engaging presenter; unusual ability to understand a profit and loss account at speed'. You'll guess the purpose of this, I'm sure: you need plenty of things in the DIFFERENT column. Discover them or create them: your choice!

The transition has been as follows:

- Stage 1: companies were hardly aware of places on the other side of the world which made things more cheaply. Shipping costs were high, communication was difficult and assumptions about low quality made them non-viable options.
- Stage 2: locations such as India, China and Taiwan became attractive for manufactured goods – clothes and toys, for example – as long as specifications were straightforward and shipping costs were not too high.
- Stage 3: communications improved sufficiently, especially via the Internet. International companies required 24–7 services. Global players had to compete in all markets and provided a demand for lower-cost services in various countries.
- Stage 4: companies started outsourcing and offshoring accounts, call centres, support services. There was some success but, not surprisingly, many organisations failed to anticipate the problems.
- Stage 5: consumer resistance – an increasingly articulated irritation at dealing with people who do not understand, cannot be understood and have no idea of the context of a question.

Implications for organisations

As always, the strategic definition is critical. What are you trying to do? Undoubtedly reduce costs, but with what parameters? Presumably not damaging the brand, for example. And what about service standards? The correct approach is, of course, to recognise what the true commodity aspects of the service are (such as handling email enquiries) but what they are definitely not (handling phone enquiries). The latter need context, clear understanding, good use of language and clear empathy. Thus 'alternative shoring' is still possible, but only when carefully and strategically done – and not on a wholesale basis.

Implications for you

Don't become a commodity. Remember that many mechanical and even decision-making skills can be replaced by technology. Keep asking yourself whether what you do could be replaced by a silicon chip. To avoid becoming a commodity become the very best at what you do. The world still needs some bank managers; not everything can be done by machine. You simply need to be one of the best. Then build your EQ or emotional intelligence skills; the ones which almost by definition a machine cannot do – leading, being empathetic or creative, innovative and inspiring. Finally, offer high RoI – return on investment. Be extraordinarily good value. That doesn't mean long hours; it simply means that what you do is done so effectively that nobody would want to lose you.

Every morning in Africa, a gazelle wakes up. It knows it must run faster than the fastest lion or it will be killed. Every morning a lion wakes up. It knows it must outrun the slowest gazelle or it will starve to death. It doesn't matter whether you are a lion or a gazelle. When the sun comes up, you better start running. African proverb

How did it go?

Q. *Isn't it true that much outsourcing is unsustainable and some organisations are returning to their former home-based business models?*

A. Yes, but once again this is a little short sighted. The big problem is the off/on, all or nothing approach too many organisations are taking. What can not be outsourced are highly evolved people skills which can take years to develop, coupled with language proficiency. If either language or soft skills or both are missing, the customer is not being valued. And they will go elsewhere.

Q. *I get the point: don't be or become a commodity. But, and it's a big but, I'm essentially a jobbing bookkeeper. There are plenty of us; what do I do?*

A. Firstly, stop thinking like that: decide you are different. Then become really different through your soft skills (being pleasant to deal with, responsive, etc.). Finally, see if you can build in some interesting extras which though small are useful – perhaps something like a highly itemised invoice. Good luck.

33. Getting it there

Manufacturing and distribution: how to make it, how to ship it. How to have the right amount of stock, just in time working, total quality management...

All you need to know but were afraid to ask.

Manufacturing

Two essential concepts have transformed this area.

■ TQM or total quality management is the concept of encouraging the whole organisation to live and breathe quality. In addition, it means recognising that 'getting things right first time' has substantial time and money savings further into any manufacturing process. The concept of TQM is surrounded by many methodologies and certification schemes but possibly the most important aspect is that it is discussed and believed in by the entire organisation.

■ JIT or just in time is the concept of having deliberately limited inventory because components arrive 'just in time' – when they are needed – rather than having them sitting around. Clearly, if that can be achieved smoothly it reduces costs, not just for the actual inventory, in that payment can be delayed, but also the critical cost of storage.

The pursuit of both ideas is strategically valuable in an organisation so long as they do not become an end in themselves. Watch out for this; classically it can turn into the pursuit of various quality certificates and sometimes, ironically, corners are cut to ensure a satisfactory 'inspection day'. That is not what they are about!

Here's an idea for you...

Consider a way you currently manufacture and/or distribute something and 'flip it' 180 degrees – then consider trying a pilot with the resulting idea. OK, here's an example. Say you are a small, specialist ice-cream manufacturer based in the UK's west country with an equally small distribution network (in comparative terms) covering just 20% of the country. You are limited by production capabilities on the farm. Could you create ice-cream-making machines which could produce ice-cream on site (in restaurants, stores, etc.), just in time? Perhaps it sounds ridiculous, but is it possible?

Two vital tools have revolutionised the processes, technology and automation. Technology essentially allows extra speed and additional accuracy. For instance, it can give you immediate information on which items in your sandwich range are popular – if any – in very hot weather, so that adjustments can be made to the products available as soon as possible. Technology then allows extensive automation. Business is about responsiveness. People can often slow things down because of fatigue, loss of concentration or simply gossiping, whereas a computer can speed it up. Automation has been an invaluable boon in areas such as barcoding and online ordering.

There are clear implications for you and/or your clients:

- Set clear quality goals and have a team accountable for quality, but ensure that the message is that 'we want real quality' and the accompanying certificates are simply the icing on the cake, and not goals in themselves.
- Steadily strip out all the slack in processes with a clear, reliable set of suppliers.
- Maximise the use of current technology. Ask IT for regular reports on what is possible and attempt to make use of new ideas immediately.
- Automate and remove human error and human foibles as thoroughly as you can. Use people for what they are good at: thinking, service, leadership…

Distribution

There are no easy rules in this area. The key is to experiment and realise that you can get almost whatever path you choose to work for you by giving it sufficient attention. Here are three good examples that illustrate this point; you'll probably be able to think of others. Some supermarkets have chosen to distribute their food which has been ordered online from central locations, while others do it from the nearest shop. Both methods seem to have their pros and cons, but both appear to be able to work. Some sandwich suppliers make their sandwiches centrally and distribute them early in the morning, while Pret a Manger has a kitchen in every shop. And a final example is how many excellent Internet companies, which have easy to use websites with prompt ordering, let themselves down with unreliable local delivery organisations. 'Distribution' is not when a piece of furniture leaves the factory; it's when your customers are unwrapping their chair in the living room thirty-six hours after having ordered it at 2.03 a.m. And they are delighted.

Let's look at the implications for you and your clients here, too. During the quality planning round, keep asking the question 'Are we distributing in the best way for us and the best way for our clients?' The answer must always be a definite 'Yes!' – of course.

Almost all quality improvement comes via simplification of design, manufacturing… layout, processes, and procedures. Tom Peters

How did it go?

Q. Where should our company be looking for manufacturing advantages?

A. Firstly, capture the manufacturing process from start to finish. Make no assumptions; seriously consider 'walking the line'. Where is ink actually added? How do the flat boxes actually get turned into 3D boxes and get taped up? Why do there seem to be so many light fittings remaining each time a run is done? The next stage is to analyse the process thoroughly and tweak everything possible. Where could a process be automated? Where could a person do three tasks instead of one and get extra pay and more interest? Where could two plants be combined? Then agree the plan, implement it and revisit it every quarter during the planning round.

Q. All right, now where should we be looking for more advantages, perhaps with automation?

A. Take the output from the analysing stage, after you've done your tweaking, and give it to your IT people. Then give it to an appropriately qualified external consultant. Identity what could be done and when, and do it quickly.

34. Risk management

It's a risky world out there, especially in the commercial sector. Companies might get forecasts wrong, fall victim to fraud or have their computers stolen…

That's just the start of the knock-on effect — but here's how to worry constructively.

What is risk?

Certainly, in English anyway, the use of the word 'risk' has always had a more formal tone to it. In everyday conversation we tend to talk more about problems than risks. So that's useful, in a way, because risk is actually a formal concept; when we talk about risk we mean something that might occur (losing that deal, running out of circuit boards for the new device, getting sued) that will have an impact on how we achieve our objectives (hitting sales targets, the release of the new computer, being involved in expensive litigation). We always measure risk as a combination of two factors: how great it is – i.e. its impact – and its probability or likelihood of occurring. Now, these latter two facts can help you assess an overall priority for a particular risk.

What are the sources of risk?

Agh! Everyone and everything; that's the big problem. Everything has a potential risk; it's where it is in the likelihood scale that matters. And the more you look, the more you will find risk. In some industries such as oil and gas, as you can imagine, the business is inherently risky. But what about the everyday office? There are lots of potential risks – unsafe electrical devices, scissors, falling off a wobbly chair,

Here's an idea for you...

Wander around your working location – even if it's just your home office – and start listing potential risks; find fifteen. Make two entries against each – impact (what effect it would have) and likelihood (the chance of it happening). Rate each on a scale from one to ten, where one is least and ten is most likely. Multiply the two scores together to get an overall priority. For instance, a restaurant kitchen area: impact of slipping on the floor is five, injury is possible; likelihood is actually low – three – because there are safety mats, so overall priority is fifteen. Tackle those with the highest overall priority first.

catching a leg on an open cupboard door, spilling hot coffee… Frightening, isn't it?

More formally, potential risk sources can be simply classed as:

- Human error, like forgetting to close a safety door or drinking while handling heavy industrial plant.
- Inherent in the nature of the business, such as working on an oil rig or long-distance driving.
- Commercial attitude, perhaps saving money by poor-quality computer screens or having a dangerous unsupervised car park.

Reducing risks

There are six basic things you can do.

1. Identify the risk. Have a two-pronged approach: firstly, educate all staff that it is their responsibility to notice and identify risk and then have a dedicated team who can follow-through on such identification and also do their own audits.

2. Prioritise. Decide how you will measure risk; I introduced a simple method of impact combined with likelihood above, so you could go for that.

3. Assign accountability of the solution. Once the risk has been identified and prioritised it then must be acted upon to reduce and/or remove it. Assign this accountability to someone specific.

4. Proper training. There are two kinds of training which are relevant here. The first is having an identification and responsibility mindset, ensuring that everyone realises that safety and/or risk management is everybody's

responsibility. Then there's best-practice execution: once good solutions have been worked out – whether it is wearing a safety hat or removing a plug at the end of a session – the best practice is followed.

5. Proper project management. The business of bringing a product or change to fruition does and should have a structured process if it is to reduce commercial risk – for example, failing to hit a date in the calendar when a product will sell particularly well. Good project management involves facts: What do we know? When will components be available? Which people can we use? What resources do we have? What confidence do we have in that supplier? It also involves methodology. Formal approaches should be used which identify dependencies and identify the critical path or route through the project which, if delayed, will cause overall delay.

6. Reporting. All incidents should be logged and reported so that everyone can learn from them and progress can be tracked.

At a personal level, be aware of how you might bring risk into an organisation, whatever you do, perhaps if you advise a client's business incorrectly. This should be addressed through maximum professionalism on your part but also appropriate insurance if relevant.

When it comes to the organisation, introduce points one to six above, especially company-wide training which stresses that everyone is responsible for identifying and diminishing risk. Ensure accurate, updated and distributed documentation.

A little risk management saves a lot of fan cleaning. Anon – a popular quote in the field of project management

How did it go?

Q. What is acceptable risk?

A. Sometimes you will need to decide this – for instance, when your sales team produce their business forecast, how much slippage can you accept? Sometimes the law will decide – extra fire exits to your roof-top artists' studio are needed, especially now you are renting it out to a group of artists. Generally, you will be able to get free initial advice; just do an Internet search for 'risk assessment' in your city and country.

Q. What is the best way to reduce risk?

A. Absolutely, definitely by a three-stage process. First, ask everyone to take ownership via education; secondly, by public identification of risks and thirdly by reporting success and failure openly within the organisation.

35. Build your brand

You have a brand whether you like it or not. It's what people say about you when you're not there...

Here's how to create the brand which is truly you, the brand you want.

Defining your brand

Your brand consists of the things people say about you when you are not present. Have a go at trying to encapsulate that now: imagine that you are not in the room and your name comes up for discussion. What might be said about you? Try capturing a few key words, maybe a sound bite or two. Perhaps things like reliable, creative, a bit of a problem attitude, ambitious, a loner? Try longer phrases: 'We should certainly be making more use of her' or 'I'd like to use him more, but he's a real liability with clients'. What would they say? Deep down, you know – so get it all down.

The brand you want

Now, what do you want it to be in the future? What are the words and maybe sound bites which come to mind here? Inspirational? A great leader? A 'can do' person? A great people coach? Thoughtful, pragmatic, caring, honest? Unique? Special? A financial wizard? A marketing superstar? How do you want to be seen? You decide – why not?

Here's an idea for you...

Think about some brands you know well, international or local. Which do you think are good brands and why? What made them a good brand? The answers to the first two questions of course are individual to you. But most people answer the third question by saying something like 'consistency coupled with organic, steady growth'. In other words, a brand takes time to develop and no amount of PR or online targeting can force feed it to us. People get suspicious if the brand is not consistent, too. So to make a good brand, be consistent and grow carefully.

Closing the gap

If you are like most people, there will be a gap to close between the two, between what you are and what you want to be. That's nothing to be concerned about. But how do you close that gap? Here are three powerful ideas which you can implement.

Firstly, realise that all good brands tend to be about giving people a positive experience, whether it's the Starbucks' brand and the idea of a third place, a Disney brand and the fun of childhood or the Harley-Davidson brand and not having to grow up, even if you are a fifty-year-old accountant. So think about the experience you want to give people. Perhaps you're an HR specialist. When people come to you, you want them to feel that they are valued and that their career is in capable hands, for example. Here's another one. Say you're a salesperson. You could change your clients' classic view of 'sleazy selling' if they meet someone who really is trying to ensure they get the best solution – you. What's the experience you want to offer?

The second idea is to realise that you may have become trapped by your job title, become trapped by the noun that describes you on your business card. Remember that you are a verb, not a noun. A noun just describes; it doesn't do. A verb does – it is all about action. No, you are not a kitchen salesperson; you sell a lifestyle, the ability to return to the kitchen and start cooking and living again. No, you are not a risk assessor; you make your company loads of money! So what's your verb, what do you actually do? What's the action you take?

The final idea is to remember it is not what you say but what you do that is important. The brands you least like, the ones you most distrust, are the ones who talk a lot, say a lot, but deliver little in reality. That's not the kind of brand you want to be. Be a brand that delivers, perhaps one that under-promises and over-delivers. That's a robust brand, a brand which can only get better.

Once you have decided the experience you want to offer and the nature of the verb that you want to become, decide to live and breathe these things immediately. And if you are in the position of leading people, a very interesting exercise is to encourage a discussion where individuals rewrite their job titles and decide what they are and what they want to become.

Carpenters bend wood. Fletchers bend arrows. Wise men fashion themselves. The Buddha

How did it go?

Q. This really doesn't feel like me. Let me check – are you saying that I need to go around 'advertising' myself, doing a bit of self-promotion and so on to establish my brand?

A. No, you certainly don't need to do that, especially if it doesn't feel like you. By definition that would be damaging your brand. No, what I'm suggesting is that there is nothing wrong with deciding more clearly what kind of image and/or impression you wish to portray – because simply by identifying it you are much more likely to create it. Having said that, there is no harm at all in keeping a file of thank yous and positive emails you have received, insisting on good points being discussed as well as weak ones at your annual review, and in knowing how to sell yourself at an interview.

Q. I find the idea of a personal brand a bit 'forced' and artificial. Is it any different to your reputation, for example?

A. Perhaps not, although in marketing terms you will know that brand is bigger than reputation, that reputation contributes to brand – but in the end it doesn't really matter. To protect your career path, slowly but surely create the personal brand you desire. Then protect it.

36. New World of Work drivers 4: abundance

How do you make money when there's too much choice? Certainly not by fighting a war on price. Time for a fourth look at the backdrop to the New World of Work.

How to cope in a world of abundance.

The context

We live in interesting times, in this New World of Work. There are so many characteristics of this world which are well articulated, such as the ever-accelerating speed of change. But one which is critical for business people – and which is less frequently expressed – is abundance, or the wealth of choice which is now available to everyone. From a competitive point of view this generally means having too much choice.

Abundance

Too much choice – that's what I mean by this term. But isn't choice good? Well, when you are the consumer: yes. But as employer or employee? Not necessarily, unfortunately. Once upon a time, in the Old World of Work, you had to beg for a current account. There were only a few places you could go in a city like London for a real Italian espresso, certain fruits were only available in certain seasons, rare books were hard to track down, and even for women – and certainly for men – many clothes were timeless whether they were jeans or evening wear.

Now, in the New World of Work, you can get a current account anywhere and decent coffee is available on every street corner. What fruit do you want, and when do you want it? Locating the rare book is easy – only the actual buying of it is difficult – and in fashion (whether that's jeans or a car) models quickly become out of date.

Is this good or is it bad? Well, it's not for any of us to say; it just is. But lots of choice means lots of competition and lots of competition means price pressure and the consequent slippery slope. So, don't just notice it: act – it's what you are doing your MBA for. Read on…

Here's an idea for you…

Think about the world of work over the next five years. Who are going to be the survivors, and who will be the thrivers? The BBC? Innocent Juices? Apple Computer? Starbucks? Barclays Bank? Singapore Airlines? Make your own personal thrive list. Who's on it and what do they have in common? I can guess – they all have and all are raising their standards. Excellent is their base point, and yours too, I trust.

Implications for organisations

How do you manage to build a viable business in a world of abundance? The key message is be distinct or be extinct. There are three simple rules. Firstly, build uniqueness into your product and/or solution. This can be 'hard' uniqueness such as a distinct feature, or it can be 'soft' uniqueness, such as excellent services. Next, never sell on price, sell on value. There is no 'definite, perfect acceptable' price. Convince your customers of the value. Finally, keep getting better. Take everything you do in the organisation and ask yourself how you can do it better. For instance:

- How can the reception area be better? Fresh flowers.
- How can our hot line be better? Open at 7.45 a.m. rather than 8.00 a.m.
- How can our marketing be better? Ban paper marketing as wasteful; change to online or conversational (on the phone).
- How can our HR be better? Give people a choice of courses to attend rather than 'mandated' ones.

Educate everyone in the organisation that any success which comes simply as a result of difference is likely to be short lived. Difference must be regularly recreated; feature X, opening hours Y, free coffee Z – none of these will last long because smart competitors will copy you. That's the key. Don't copy: stay ahead.

Implications for you

How do you stay employable in an abundant world? How do you ensure that your clients will still need you in a world of shuffling rivals? Here are three rules again.

- Build your personal brand: that's what people say about you when you are not present. Think what they probably say now, think what you would like them to say, and close the gap.
- Keep getting better; take everything you do and be just that little bit better at it. For example, be at your desk and ready for work at 9.00 a.m. rather than taking your coat off and complaining about the buses being late at 9.07 a.m.; contribute to meetings rather than sitting at the back with your arms folded and help customers rather than saying 'you need another department'.
- Finally, do not worry about what other people think; they are frightened by your new-found enthusiasm and desire to be better at what you do. Don't let their cynicism bring you down.

And in a nutshell?

- Don't stagnate: that's effectively going backwards.
- Don't copy: at best you just keep up.
- Jump and get ahead: that's how you survive in a world of abundance.

'Choice. The problem is choice'. Neo, in *The Matrix Reloaded*

How did it go?

Q. I'm a brand new graduate. I really have no chance to apply some of your ideas until I learn a lot more, otherwise where does my value come from?

A. Well, value is not just knowledge – it is the ability to ask questions, to be supportive, to be inspirational, to be excellent at customer service, to be able to think outside the box. You can offer incredible value now as long as you choose to do so. Never underestimate the value of your approach, your style, your soft skills. Plenty of business people have plenty of knowledge but are not able to truly realise it, but you can and will.

Q. Won't the perception of what is excellent keep changing – essentially keep going up?

A. Yes, indeed. Remind yourself what we used to accept from our banks, coffee shops, dentists, employers… They may none of them be perfect now but all of them have raised their standards considerably. They'll have to continue to do so, too; one aspect of excellence is continuously raising your standards which is easy to do, in many ways, as you are constantly investing in yourself.

37. Influencing and negotiation

Wouldn't life be easier if people recognised your genius at interview? Sadly, they don't (yet). Wouldn't it be helpful if you could get sales to work with marketing? Fat chance…

How to convince — one step at a time — and get it to stick.

When you start working on your own MBA, you enter a whole new world, one of leadership, of big business, of deals. Of strategic missions. And ego.

Oh, yes, sometimes massive ego – and, funnily enough, at times it might be yours! The smarter you get, the more knowledge you gain, the better you can sometimes get at arguing why you are right. But think about it: on your MBA journey so far you have discovered so many varying opinions. You know there are no definites; most of the MBA world is in fact about shades of grey. What you need to get good at is coping with that, of being able to agree even though you may well disagree, of being able to work with people even if you don't like each other. That's the skill of influencing and negotiation. Edward De Bono – the lateral thinking guy – once said that a sign of intelligence was the ability to hold two opposing ideas in the head at the same time. That's what you've got to get good at.

Now for ten guidelines to great influencing and negotiation. Sales and marketing are at war. The interviewer wants to start you at the bottom of the salary scale… that's when you use these guidelines.

1. Great influencing means
- Being clear on what you want. A clear goal is essential – say you want a grade B in the salary round. Couple that with a clear understanding of why you want it and it might mean that you can be flexible and agree a grade C plus a train season ticket.
- Plan, do, review. Plan your approach. Do it and then learn from it.

2. Great influencing also means:
- Understanding the other person. Always work to understand their point of view; never judge or assume.
- Respecting them. They will be different in approach and view; that's why you are negotiating. Respect those differences.
- Thinking in the long term. It's highly likely that you are going to need to work with this person again in the future; bear that in mind.

3. In addition, great influencing means paying attention to the small stuff. Choose the time, choose the place and ensure they can spare enough time.

4. You can't negotiate until you have sold; negotiation is not a way to sell. You must make sure the other person is seriously considering you for the job or the client really wants to buy a week's consultancy from you before you get into the true negotiation.

Here's an idea for you…

This is perfect for a team meeting, either with your own team or one of your clients. Tell them that they are going to be involved in a pitch to win a huge amount of business, and the pitch is them versus their major competitor – but in order to ensure they win the business the exercise is to practise the pitch as if they were the competition. After the initial shock (and it has to be said, probable complaining), the skill of getting (respectfully) into the mind of another is amazingly useful. Have fun.

5. Don't give unless you get. Attach every give to a get. 'I'd be happy to forgo the car as long as I got XXX…'

6. Give small. You may be able to give the client 25% discount, but they will appreciate it more if you don't give it all in one go. Start with 7% and work up.

7. Give slow. Similarly, get them to work for their concessions – and then they will appreciate them more.

8. Give odd. A discount of 7% is more credible than one of 10%.

9. Next year, go back to zero. Be wary – concessions are often generalised so don't allow that and insist that concessions are specific to an occasion. Just because they have 17% discount currently, does not mean they should have 17% in the next financial year.

10. Agree there and then. Don't walk out of the door with any potential confusion; draft the agreement at the time.

You can't dig a different hole by digging the same one deeper. Edward De Bono

How did it go?

Q. *I'm going to be selfish. I want more money; I want an increase in salary. Exactly how do I get that?*

A. A great question – because people do often think that this is about some clever negotiation trick, but it's not. Well, maybe a little. The way you get a great salary increase? Truly, honestly? By being really, really good at your job. So get great at your job and make sure whoever decides about your salary knows that. That's how 95% of your effort should be applied. In addition be confident at the salary interview and do not be afraid to remind them of your worth. Do those two things and you will get the salary you want and deserve.

Q. *In our sector, it just keeps coming back to price. Much of this negotiation stuff is OK if you are selling something like oil rigs. But office furniture, no way. Isn't that so?*

A. That's exactly what the oil rig sales teams say, of course: 'In this sector there are only one or two customers, so we can't really negotiate.' It's something to do with 'the grass is always greener', I think. Well, you can always negotiate, but you must create difference between you and the competition whether it's between your furniture or your CV. No difference, and you are fighting on price – and you will not win. There are three areas to create difference: your company, your product and you. Make the most of all of them.

38. How to be an entrepreneur

The world needs entrepreneurs. The world needs constant, fresh money-making ideas. Whether you head up marketing or facility management or run your own business, here's how to be an entrepreneur.

It's a careful combination of thinking and action.

The New World of Work brings many challenges created by seven drivers of change:

- Driver 1: acceleration. This is the increasing rate of change in the very different commercial world of today.
- Driver 2: automation. This is the move to replace any possible process with a chip; to go high-tech rather than high-touch.
- Driver 3: alternative shores. There is always somewhere cheaper in the world. And with the advent of the Internet and the global market 'alternative shoring' is now a valid possibility.
- Driver 4: abundance. So much choice – and in everything, from mortgages to vegetables.
- Driver 5: ambiguity. The death of long-term planning, and the unreliability of planning in general.
- Driver 6: anarchy. Power is back with the people – the Internet, rising qualifications, one market…
- Driver 7: adrenaline. Fear – accumulate the above six drivers and you end up with a world of anxiety – or potentially do so!

You'll only survive in the New World of Work if you are entrepreneurial. To be an entrepreneur is to remember that ultimately it is down to you: if there ever really was any long-term security there certainly isn't now – it's the Wild West all over again. Time to look at some detail on how exactly you can become entrepreneurial in order to survive in the future.

Mindset: how you think

Entrepreneurs think in a certain kind of way, and everyone can borrow that kind of thinking.

- Adding value. Entrepreneurs know that one aspect of differentiation and making money is through distinction, through being different and that it can be done by adding value. They discover what their customers want – longer opening hours, less packaging, more crisps in the bag – and do their best to give it to them.

- No failure, only feedback. Entrepreneurs know that the world is too complicated to be able to plan and get everything right first time – or ever – so they are willing to try things and, if they go wrong, to learn and improve.

- There's always a way! Breakthroughs so often come when attention is given to what everybody else said couldn't be done – entrepreneurs recognise this.

- 'We can make this better.' Entrepreneurs believe in *kaizen*: never-ending continuous improvement.

- Qualifications do not (necessarily) equal success. Entrepreneurs realise that – whether or not they are graduates, have MBAs or left school as soon as they could – being an entrepreneur in the New World of Work is a state of mind and not a qualification-rich CV. The latter can help, but it can also hinder. And that goes for worrying about other aspects, like your sex, age, skin colour, creed, height…

Here's an idea for you…

Take a product you use a lot (your mobile, your kettle, your car, your washing machine). What's a frustration you have with it? There's bound to be something; your mobile's battery needs constant recharging; your kettle gets hard-water stains; your car has two serious blind spots and your washing machine has too many options… Now ask outrageous questions. What would it take to create a phone that never needed charging, a kettle that couldn't stain, brand new cars configured to remove all blind spots or a three-option washing machine? You're thinking seriously about it, aren't you? That's your entrepreneurial spirit – get it to work.

159

Mechanics: what you do

How do entrepreneurs become good at their craft? By doing it. Be in no doubt: start something; start a small online business for additional income, reinvent your HR department. Keep asking the question 'If this were my own thing, how would I be managing it differently?' For instance, 'If my department were involved in a management buy-out, would it be a natural survivor?' Once you do that you will learn rapidly. Work hard to reduce any external dependencies so that you are not dependent on good market conditions or a favourable supplier, or vulnerable to a downturn or the loss of a market. That's great entrepreneurial action.

External/internal: the two aspects

There are, perhaps, two main kinds of entrepreneurs: those who are out there in the wilderness attempting to get their purest of juices established or their new totally biological organic nappies sold through the main supermarkets, and those who are within organisations. These are the people who realise that heading a fifteen-person support team was sustainable in profitable, great-product-margin days but is not so good when the economy is in a bit of a squeeze.

> The critical ingredient is getting off your butt and doing something. It's as simple as that. ... The true entrepreneur is a doer, not a dreamer.

Nolan Bushnell, American Atari Computer entrepreneur

How did it go?

Q. I'm sorry, but surely the true entrepreneur is born?

A. Nature or nurture, genes or upbringing? There is no doubt that some individuals have a feel and bent for entrepreneurial thinking. You must nurture your nature, work hard to become the best version of you – and you can develop it, be in no doubt. The two vital areas are mindset adjust your thinking – and practice.

Q. How can I get my clients and the people in my team to be more entrepreneurial?

A. The best way is to model such behaviours yourself and show that you are willing to break down some of the boundaries and think in some different ways – maybe you are willing (in some of your work) to be paid by results, for example. Radical? Yes, of course. But high impact? Certainly! Once you've established that, create some specific projects which require entrepreneurial thinking, like turning a cost centre department into a profit centre.

39. Why are you doing an MBA anyway?

Stop. Take a walk. Why are you doing this? Let's talk it through, together.

'If you know why you want something, you are more likely to get it.' Think about that.

You are ahead of the game: you are managing your own MBA. That gets you flexibility (of curriculum, of time). It saves you money and allows you to ease yourself into the real thing, if that is what you fancy doing later on. Even so, it's worth examining – what is it about those three magic letters? And if you know why, you really are more likely to get it.

Here's what I mean. You've taken up archery and love it. Obviously, initially – for good safety reasons – you are confined to the indoor range. But eventually your coach says you are ready for the outside world. You go outside, eager with anticipation. Your coach stands back and says 'Go for it; fire a few arrows'. You look around, feeling a little silly. 'Er – where's the target?' 'Oh,' says your coach, 'we don't do targets.' And you think, where's the fun in that? The moral of the tale? No target: no results. So let's look at some MBA targets.

Why do an MBA?

- 'I will make more money.' Possibly, not necessarily. The first 'MBAers' were rare people, so they were highly desirable and could command higher salaries. But, as you are aware, the MBA is rapidly becoming a commodity. Some employers have even – shock, horror – begun to say they don't want 'MBAers'. So you probably shouldn't do any form of MBA just to get a salary increase. There are probably easier ways, such as doing an astounding job in your own organisation and getting promotion.

- 'I will be more marketable.' That's probably true. MBA thinking and study is much more aligned to the business world than first and general degrees. Equally, it requires higher levels of rigour – for instance, in analysis and critical thinking – which is valuable. That's probably a good reason for doing a formal MBA and certainly for managing your own MBA as you are now doing.

- 'I want prestige.' It will give you that to a certain extent, especially if you can get into the right school. But it's a lot of time and money if you just simply want to feel good about having gained an MBA. You can get prestige in other ways: a successful, well-read blog, for example. This is probably not a good reason if it is your only one.

- 'I want time to think.' Certainly this will be the case, but talk to past students and you will discover that you do have to work to get that time; otherwise you will find you are busy and time can rush by. But with good time discipline, yes,

Here's an idea for you...

Ask your local business school if you can do some research which you will happily share with them. You would like permission to email their MBA graduates from five, three and one years ago, and you would like to ask two simple questions. The first is this: 'Before you started your MBA what did you see as the top benefit?' and the other is 'With the benefit of hindsight, what do you see as the top benefit?' Keep it really simple as you'll have a lot of qualitative results to go through. From experience, my prediction would be before: money; after: thinking and reflection. Something for you to think about!

you can get time to think in an environment which actively encourages that. A great reason – and one which managing your own MBA really encourages, of course.

- 'I want to build my value.' Yes, another great reason. You will build your value and you will feel more confident in your value.

- 'I want to become smarter.' And another great reason. You'll develop your thinking, particularly your critical thinking, and you will become smarter.

- 'I want to do something different but I am not sure what.' Mmm. Maybe. Maybe a month off would give you the reflection time you need? (And maybe you should try an extended break before launching on to a busy academic year.) After all, the MBA gives a very blinkered view of 'something different' and, despite what people think, few MBA courses are really hot on career guidance.

- 'My company pays for me.' Now, this is a tricky one. It's almost too easy and how can you turn down such an opportunity? I really – in the nicest possible way – hope you have to fight to get a place. You don't? Well, I suggest you pretend you do: write a 500-word application on why you want to do one. Otherwise, there's no real passion and no real results.

I'm going to scrap the MBA. In an age of creativity–design–innovation, who wants to be a 'Master' of 'Administration'? Master of 'Paper Pushing'? Computers do that. Tom Peters

How did it go?

Q. *So is the MBA dead?*

A. Increasingly so, as the 'increase your salary by at least 50%' product. But for reflection, building value, reinventing, it's as good as ever. However, when you examine those reasons for doing it, you realise that there are others which might provide even better options, such as taking a year out, such as a long holiday or such as switching career dramatically for a year or two.

Q. *But you have to agree that an MBA is on the 'tick list' for some jobs?*

A. Yes. Sometimes rightly, sometimes wrongly. If you do really need one, get one as quickly and as efficiently as possible. Show you are top MBA material at the interview but never assume anything: check that an MBA really is mandatory for the job/career you want. Maybe the company just wants people with great presence, self-starters, people who have done the work themselves. Someone like you, maybe? Then it's not about the formal MBA, it's about selling yourself. You can do that.

40. How to do research and produce a white paper

Even if you don't do the full MBA, this is an invaluable skill: research a subject, strip out the padding, summarise the essentials and produce an executive summary.

Invaluable for you, brilliant for others — here's how.

Once upon a time, in some parts of the world, school language teachers would make their pupils undergo a particularly unpleasant (for most, anyway) ritual: writing a précis. A précis was reducing the word count of a text but without losing its essential meaning. Often it was a newspaper article (which wasn't too bad, knowing the amount of 'waffle' in the writing of some journalists) or a couple of pages from a formal textbook. It was tough but valuable. However, these days you are unlikely to have been taught that skill at school, or seen it coached anywhere, but in today's busy, busy, busy world, it is probably one of the most useful skills around. It's called the executive summary or white paper, and I'll define it as a convenient summary of all that needs to be known on a subject.

Why a white paper is so useful
- Busyness: busy people appreciate accessible, readable and summarised information.

- Attention: if it is short and relevant it is likely to get read.
- Prioritisation: 'short and sweet' allows something to be given the priority it needs.
- 'Single and same view': a group of people can be brought up to speed very quickly.
- Deepens understanding: the production (as opposed to the receipt) of a white paper can have a powerful benefit in aiding the true understanding of a subject.

All of these are vital, of course, in quality MBA work. The quality of the communication must be 'owned' by the originator of the work, too, mind. For instance, a long and rambling email should simply not be sent, especially if it's gone to lots of people. The sender of that email has just saved maybe ten minutes by not editing it, but they have wasted the time and possibly even confused the (many) recipients. Own your communication and ask that of your team and clients, as well.

Producing a white paper
Here are eight basic points which will help you.

1. State: you need to be 'in a great state': calm and focused is good. Generally don't attempt to produce one when you are tired or stressed, or both.
2. Read and immerse yourself in your subject: start the reading process and resist the attempt to produce your summary too soon. Take notes and make reminders of sources as you read – it can be very fiddly to do the latter afterwards.

Here's an idea for you...
At your next team meeting, use the following powerful exercise; you'll need laptops. Brief the group as follows: 'We need to get a concise and agreed picture of the current competitive situation. You have thirty minutes to write as much as you can.' Get people to write/brainstorm and capture their individual view. The emphasis is on quantity. At the end of the time, get them to state their word count, then ask them to reduce this by half. Give them fifteen minutes. Now ask everyone to read their output and then produce their final version. This tends to produce a high-quality summary of the current competitive situation in addition to readying minds for further work.

3. Read deep; really get into that subject. Never see depth as a waste of time. The deeper you go into a subject the more your basic understanding improves.

4. Read wide; be willing to expand. Strategy needn't just be 'commercial', it could be military, too. Deep insights are often formed as you go wide.

5. Incubate. Leave your reading for a day or two and let your brain work on it in the background.

6. Write once. Sit down and write, and attempt to do this in one sitting.

7. Précis: now edit it to your required length and 'substance'.

8. Structure: if you are making your white paper formal, then consider structuring it at least as follows:

- Executive summary: 200 words at most which give the 'very essence' of the subject.
- Relevant data: the facts of the case, the 'hard data' you can rely on.
- Conclusion: make what you are suggesting clear.
- References: so you can back up your claims and so others can pursue the points if they wish to do so.

Any darn fool can make something complex; it takes a genius to make something simple.

Pete Seeger, musician and political activist

How did it go?

Q. *How formal should I be when producing a piece of research?*

A. If it is for internal use in your company then you probably need go no further than a simple note of your sources. This is important for credibility and if you want to further pursue a point. If you are attempting to submit your work to a journal, perhaps the *Harvard Business Review*, then you will find that they have a detailed checklist of things that are necessary (including structure and appearance) for submission. Break these rules and you won't be considered.

Q. *I can't say my writing skills are that great, but some of my colleagues haven't written anything since they were at school and it's going to take ages. Is doing this a good use of their time?*

A. The writing of an article or 'executive summary' does require that all your ideas be processed, validated, connected and summarised. These are all essential skills in business nowadays so, yes, it's a valuable use of their time. But, as with the development of any skill, it'll take time to develop. Give it that time and the pay-off will be huge.

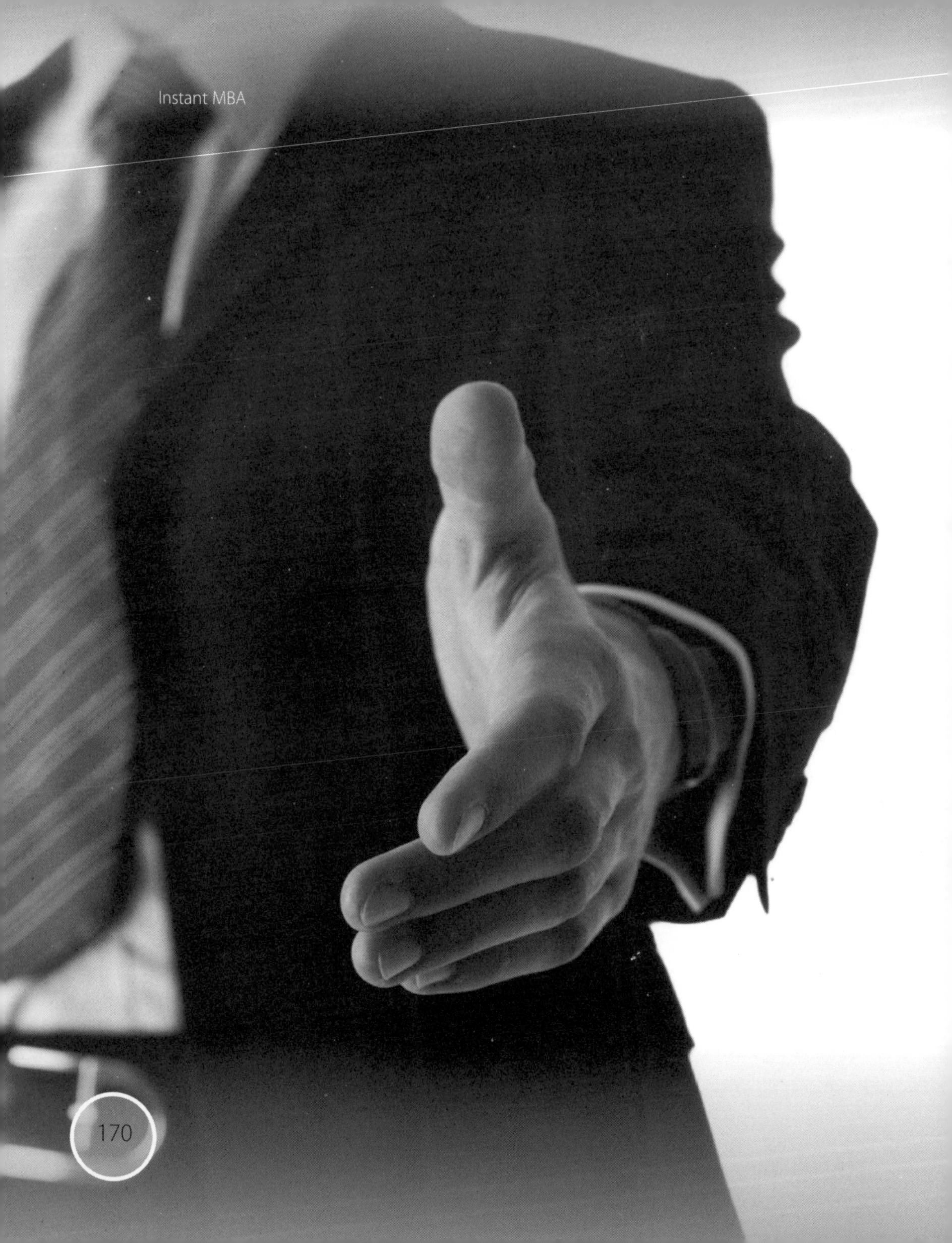

41. Know your thought leader 5: Daniel Goleman

Daniel Goleman? Not usually on the business school list...

But if there is one bit of feedback the business community keeps giving to the business schools it is this: we need people with great interpersonal skills.

That's Goleman's field: emotional intelligence – and it's your secret weapon. Daniel Goleman is an author, a consultant, a scientist and a psychologist whose main 'thing' is emotional intelligence, on which he has written many books and articles. He is not purely an academic and is not attached to any particular university although he has been a visiting lecturer at Harvard. As well as being an author he spends a large part of his time on the lecture circuit. His most famous and probably most widely read book is *Emotional Intelligence*.

What is emotional intelligence?
Let's keep this definition very simple: it's the ability to notice and hence vary your emotions and to use that ability to be more effective. For example, you are discussing a new contract with a client and discover that they are trying to reduce the fee they will pay to you significantly; you find that this fact is annoying

Here's an idea for you...

Think about the fields of expertise you enjoy – sport, business or music, perhaps. In any of those fields, think of some people you admire. Now think about what it is that you admire about them and try to divide what you admire into technical/functional (hard) or emotional (soft) competencies. You probably noticed that those you admire in your chosen fields have strong technical or functional skills, such as the ability to pay a cello with elegance. But those you particularly admire have excellent interpersonal skills, too – perhaps an appropriate level of humility or a skill in developing others… that's emotional intelligence.

you. As you notice that feeling of annoyance you also notice that you are feeling less effective. So you suggest that it might be useful to take a break; on returning you are more focused and able to resolve the issue positively. That's emotional intelligence in action. Oh, and it's often abbreviated to EQ – the emotional equivalent of IQ.

Why is it important in business?

Well, business is about relationships and relationships are about emotional intelligence. Anything which helps forge stronger, more effective relationships has got to be good for business. And IQ – i.e. linguistic and numerical intelligence – is generally considered to be fixed, but emotional intelligence can be developed. Used wisely, this can give your business a distinct competitive advantage.

Personal emotional intelligence

Those things, of course, apply to you as an individual as well as to your business. In addition, most people pursue what you might call happiness or contentment. Being able to manage and use emotions effectively contributes in large part to that happiness or contentment. You can generally improve your emotional intelligence by, firstly, understanding its components and, secondly, by practising those components. So let's look at them.

There are generally considered to be five levels of emotional intelligence. I'll define each and then show how it can be developed. Now, there are several models of emotional intelligence in existence; the one which follows is most closely modelled on Goleman's work.

1. Self-awareness: the ability to notice your own emotions, to notice that you are angry or pensive or fearful, perhaps. This ability is best developed through 'soft skills' training courses, reading widely and seeking regular, honest feedback.

2. Self-regulation: the ability to choose your response, maybe to choose to ignore a sarcastic comment because you realise the person was feeling a bit tired and is not being deliberately malicious. This is best developed by investing time in yourself, most simply by taking breaks during the day.

3. Self-motivation: the ability to see a higher picture, to be motivated to choose the 'best' emotion at the time – for example, being empathetic when it might be tempting to be angry. This is best developed by articulating your vision, your longer-term view of where life is going and developing.

4. Empathy: the ability to relate to another person, such as to understand the client's perspective. This is best developed by spending time understanding the views of another person, seeking to understand and not judging too quickly.

5. Interpersonal skills: developing a portfolio of skills such as rapport or assertiveness which can be used at the appropriate times.

For star performance... emotional competence is twice as important as purely cognitive abilities.

Daniel Goleman

173

How did it go?

Q. I am committed to working on my own emotional intelligence and attempting to improve it. How can I encourage others in my organisation to do so, too?

A. The most effective way seems to be to model or adopt the behaviours you are seeking in someone yourself. In general, unless you have excellent trust or rapport with someone, they are unlikely to simply accept being 'told' the behaviours you want. However if you use them yourself on a day-to-day basis other people will notice the significant increase in effectiveness which you have. They may realise why or ask why – either way, you are creating the change you seek.

Q. But surely some things about us just, well, are. You know, moods, temperament, things like that. What about if you just have a bad day?

A. Wooahh! A few things rolled into one there, I think… Yes – we just 'are' in the sense that our genes dictate a lot about us; you mention things such as temperament. Research does suggest that people have differing thresholds for boredom, anger, even happiness. But the work of Goleman and many others does give us hope that we can manage those aspects of our nature or, to put it a little more elegantly, that we can nurture our nature. Take any aspect and try it; you'll see it works.

42. Know your thought leader 6: Jim Collins

The 'good to great' man. He's had a big influence on a lot of businesses identifying essential success factors for and articulating so-called 'level five' leadership.

So: what's the theory and does it work?

So, who is James C. Collins, generally referred to as Jim Collins? He is an author, a consultant and a lecturer on business sustainability. He is not purely an academic and is not attached to any particular university although he has a 'management laboratory' in Boulder, Colorado. As well as being an author he spends a large part of his time on the lecture circuit. His most famous and probably most widely read book is *Built to Last*. He is most definitely a major thought leader to include as you study for your instant MBA.

Many people have found his work to be a refreshing change; he articulates much which appears to be common sense and goes more for the general case rather than the special one. In the field of leadership, for instance, the concept of the charismatic 'rock-star' leader has become familiar – but often that seems not to be essential; it's just a special case. Deliberately seeking or trying to create that kind of leadership may, therefore, be a mistake. What can you learn from Jim Collins? Well, there are two valid strands to his work: business suitability and leadership. Clearly the two are strongly interrelated, but let's look at them in turn.

Here's an idea for you...

Leadership. Now there's a topic. But take a moment. Forget anyone's research. List every leader you've ever had – from school, sports, whatever. What made them leadership material? Their charisma or their diligence and humility? Did you get evidence to support both? Now add some of your favourite leaders from the wider world. Does it distort the picture? A bit, because these are public figures, and maybe they are public figures because of their charisma. There are undoubtedly both kinds of leaders, but perhaps more leaders than you think are just quiet, hard-working people.

Business Sustainability: *Built to Last* and *Good to Great*

Here are a selection of essentials from these two books:

- Be a Clock Builder not a Timekeeper – potentially confusing terms to the outsider, instilled with time-management jargon. This is simply saying get your company to run smoothly, as smooth as clockwork. Clearly this saves time and energy and allows a focus on things which couldn't have been anticipated.

- BHAGs (big hairy audacious goals). You've no doubt heard this term and wondered where it came from. It's self-explanatory: have something so amazing ('put a man on the moon' stuff) that it galvanises people.

- Develop a cult-like culture, one which people love and want to maintain. A certain 'way of doing things around here'. This is something which is special to your company.

- Look inside for leadership, especially at the top. Anyone who has worked in an organisation knows this frustration: external candidates always seem better – and that is, of course, because you don't really know them. Choose from inside; these people are much more likely to be the best candidates in the long term.

- No dynamic leaders. Ah: interesting. Leadership, but not necessarily 'charismatic' leadership.

- No great initial idea. Another interesting one; you don't need the next iPhone to start your company.
- 'Right people on the bus.' This is a lovely term for great recruitment. You can't face this problem later; it's too late.
- Face reality. Don't hide from market or product problems.

Leadership: level 5 leadership

Collins defined the level 5 leaders as having two great qualities: professional will and personal humility. Both of these are, of course, accessible to all of us, whereas 'charisma' is perhaps more of a stretch. That's great news: stop playing at being a 'rock star' and get on with some work. Easy, really! And if you are wondering why 'level 5', here is the full hierarchy in brief: level 1: highly capable individual (knowledge plus skills plus habits); level 2: contributing team member (team player); level 3: competent manager (organiser); level 4: effective leader (catalyst) and, finally, level 5 (humility plus will).

If I were running a company today, I would have one priority above all others: to acquire as many of the best people as I could. I'd put off everything else to fill my bus. Jim Collins

How did it go?

Q. Pardon me, but yet another theory? How come it's better than any other?

A. It isn't, necessarily. In support of Jim Collins, he is a careful researcher and so you can probably have more confidence in his data than most. On the other hand – as you would expect – he has plenty of critics. In particular, Tom Peters constantly points out (with significant truth, it has to be said) that any organisation which sets out to be permanent is doomed – as in today's New World of Work the organisation must be incredibly flexible. To paraphrase Peters: sometimes it's best if a company simply has to reinvent itself and start again.

Q. I run a tiny organisation. When I look at some of these concepts, they seem to imply that a large organisation is essential. Does that mean that I can only be sustainable if I become larger?

A. No, certainly don't pick up that message. Collins is very keen on research and in many ways it's easier to do research on larger organisations – but what is probably true is that you must 'get big or get niche or get out'. In other words, size does bring business benefits, but its big downfall is losing specialisms: that's to your advantage. If you have specialisms now, keep them; what often happens as an organisation grows is that it loses what makes it special in the race to build revenue and market share. Don't let this happen to you.

43. Tutorial 2 – application in the 'real world'

Time for another tutorial (think I'd leave out one of the best aspects of the course?)… It's on a tricky topic – application and relevance to reality.

Who'd like to start?

At this point in your MBA, you've probably assimilated plenty of ideas already. You know, a bit of Michael Porter, some Peter Drucker, a touch of Just In Time… and the rest. That would be OK but – and it's a big but – how do you actually apply this stuff in the real business world, especially when some of the key ideas appear to oppose each other? Perhaps I can pull it together in this tutorial, using tips from other successful students.

Tip 1: It's not as easy as it looks, is it?
The challenge with so many management books is that everything looks so easy and straightforward. In fact, applying the ideas is often tough; very tough. Here's how to do it.
- As you read, make notes or highlight (or both) practical application statements. Most current authors do create more practical sections in their books – they'd not have much credibility if they didn't. Distil the book from management text into field guide.

■ Really understand that field guide, and apply it.

■ Notice if/how it works and be willing to review the ideas.

■ Then write to the authors via their blogs seeking clarification of any points.

■ Pay for an hour of a professor's time at your local university, and ask specifically for a 'theory into action' conversation.

Tip 2: Opposites attract...

Dealing with ideas that are simply opposing – when what one author says is the opposite of what another says – can mean you feel like a rabbit caught in the headlights. It's a tricky one, this, so let's think it through.

Often what appear to be opposing ideas are simply the respective authors addressing different aspects of the same continuum of thinking. A good example is 'big is powerful' versus 'small is beautiful'. Are these opposing ideas? No; they are both true. If an organisation becomes large it has all the benefits of market presence, buying power, lower costs of sale, etc.; if an organisation deliberately stays small it has the benefits of attractiveness in its niche, being nimble, etc.

The reality is that often the author is saying 'give attention to my idea'. And when you give attention to something, it tends to work (remember the Hawthorne effect?). So the best strategy is to find the methodology which best fits with your experience and plans and follow it fully: give it massive attention. It will then work

---

Here's an idea for you...

Gather three colleagues from work; four of you in total. Each of you should prepare a five-minute reading from a business book, followed by asking a question based on that reading. The rest of you then attempt to answer the question, facilitated by the reader. After a total of fifteen minutes per person, move on to the next. So you might read a paragraph on pricing strategy and then ask 'How does that help us make more money?' This can be great fun and you will run out of time, but keep it that way: short, sharp, fast. And look forward to another session.

for you. Just bear in mind – a little cynically, perhaps – that any guru/author/thought leader knows that one way to get a bit of publicity for their ideas is to be controversial. Hence they love disagreeing with an apparently well-established or 'given' idea.

Tip 3: One formula for success?

You'd think it was possible to find a summarised formula for business success – it surely ought to exist, with everything which has been written on the subject. How many business books are generated each week? How many strategy books? How many leadership books? How many gurus are 'launched' every year? We should all have learned something about business by now, so let me try and summarise:

- A strategy is good. Too many organisations – let's be honest – do not actually know what they are doing nor why they are doing it. So, get a strategy. Is there a perfect, definitive one? No, just get one.
- The strategy should be based on the best current thinking for your business, the market you are in and current political and economic factors.
- Turn that strategy into a plan with actions, milestones and full accountabilities.
- Execute that plan.
- Learn from the execution; review and improve.
- Repeat that cycle at regular intervals.

In the development of intelligence nothing can be more 'basic' than learning how to ask productive questions.

Neil Postman, academic, critic and author of *Amusing Ourselves to Death*

How did it go?

Q. Don't you consider it odd that most 'successful' business people do not have much of an academic background and certainly don't do an MBA?!

A. Well, remember that what you're doing with your instant MBA is a highly successful compromise between the academic world of higher education – which can sometimes have a disconnect with the world of business – and the business person who is entirely self-taught. I'm not saying that doing an MBA will make you successful or an excellent business person. I am saying that applying the ideas you study makes you highly likely to become so. Some are born with those ideas, people like Richard Branson; the rest of us (you and me) need to learn them.

Q. You knew this was coming. What is the Hawthorne effect you mentioned earlier?

A. It describes the temporary change in behaviour and/or performance in response to a change in environmental conditions; the response usually being a change for the good. Basically, pay attention to something and you'll notice an improvement. The term was coined by Henry A. Landsberger when analysing experiments from 1924–1930 at the Hawthorne Works outside Chicago.

44. New World of Work drivers 5: ambiguity

Another detailed look at the background to the New World of Work – this time it's ambiguity: the inability to be predictable. That's what it is; uncertainty is what people feel.

How do you lead in a world of ambiguity? How do you lead when you feel uncertain? Read on.

Setting it in context

'The New World of Work' is a handy term for the world of work, as it is now. About ten years ago things began to change significantly; among other things, there was an increasing tendency towards 'ambiguity' or an inability to plan and be certain – it is the fifth of the seven drivers of change. It had been quite different in the Old World of Work. Of course, 'ambiguity' has been around in business for a while; in the New World of Work it's simply concerned with the increasing difficulty of strategic planning and being sure that any 'winning' strategy will be a certain one.

Ambiguity

Things were once a lot less ambiguous, a lot more predictable. Here are some examples.

■ Who sells mortgages? Once upon a time, only certain key financial institutions. That's not so now; more and more organisations can provide you with a mortgage. Is this good? Is it bad? No – it just is.

Here's an idea for you...

Ask as many people as you can the following questions: What do you dislike? What do you hate? What worries you most? You'll get answers as far ranging as 'giving presentations', 'global warming' or 'people who fiddle their expenses'. Then ask a follow-up question about what it is that causes that feeling. Why don't they like giving presentations? What is it that concerns them about global warming? The ultimate answer is usually the lack of certainty.

- Who are you speaking to? Once you would exchange information face to face, on the phone or perhaps via a letter. With the Internet, you are a lot less certain who you are speaking to. Security – in all its aspects – has become a major issue.
- Who are you buying from? Once upon a time it was the producers themselves; now, increasingly, products and services are outsourced. Again, it's neither good nor bad; it's how things are.
- Your competitors. Once they were visible, 'targetable'. That's no longer the case.
- Whether a product is good or bad. It would once have a seal or a crest or an 'established in 1912'. Not now. Products may come and go, but can still be excellent while they are around.

And as a consequence of the above (and, of course, a whole lot more of the same) everyone feels uncertain.

Uncertainty

It seems that we human beings need and crave a certain amount of certainty, stability and security. Whether you study the work of Abraham Maslow or Martin Seligman you'll know there are certain things we need to be happy, from roofs over our heads to food to fulfilling jobs. Yes, it's that latter which can cause concerns. What if your job is not secure? Your job is fundamental to your happiness. Whatever theory you subscribe to, your job and career provide the most basic things (money for food and shelter), the most essential ones (an ability to fulfil our talents) and the most subtle ones, too (a definition of who you are). No wonder a world of ambiguity gives people the shudders.

The implications for organisations

- The death of long-term planning. No longer is it possible to create the long-term plans so beloved of the marketing strategists. That doesn't mean you shouldn't attempt to do so, but you must be aware that they are a whole lot more unreliable.
- The need for an alert rapid response team. You must create a team who are constantly updating those plans; effectively the planning round becomes once a month rather than once a quarter.
- The need for education and a 'back to the Wild West' feeling. Without removing the organisation's need to be effective employers, you must educate your employees that the new security lies in them developing their own skills, resilience and effectiveness, and not in leaving that to the organisation.

The implications for you

There are two basic areas. The first is the need for a broader and longer-term plan than you currently have. Create a bigger vision of where you want to take your career and ask yourself the blunt question: will those jobs still be around? Then there's the need for an entrepreneurial mindset. Decide that you are running your own business and will start investing in yourself.

I tore myself away from the safe comfort of certainties through my love for truth – and truth rewarded me. Simone de Beauvoir

How did it go?

Q. What are the secure business areas nowadays?

A. Anyone who knows the answer to that question is lying! In a world of ambiguity it is increasingly hard to define what a successful business proposition will be. However, in the foreseeable future, there are three likely trends for success. One is taking the current situation and making it 'better', such as reducing cash withdrawal time on an ATM. The second is recognising the growth areas which are still leisure, home expenditure, etc. The final one is watching for brand new emerging markets, perhaps a population which is increasingly aging, but fit and healthy, and thinking about how that market can be serviced.

Q. You referred to Maslow and Seligman earlier. Why are they important?

A. The work of both Abraham Maslow and Martin Seligman is concerned with what 'turns us on', what motivates us and makes us happy. As marketers and business people this is of essential interest because if we can align with such thinking we can ensure our product's success. Maslow created a famous hierarchy of needs which said we had a need for shelter at the base level, and that at the top level we needed to become 'self-actualised' or to release our full potential. Seligman addressed the question of what makes us happy and discovered that it's not necessarily 'stuff', but more our relationships and career.

45. Reinvent. Regularly

One of the major banks said recently: 'if we were launching today, there is absolutely, categorically no way we would design a bank like this'. So what's to be done? Reinvent...

How to turn around a business: rapidly. New, struggling or failing — you are the person to do it.

Stage 1: review the 'hot spots'

- Hot spot 1: marketing. Review the '4 Ps': product, price, place and promotion. Ask yourself the tough questions: what's the product, who are our customers, how will we talk to them and why are we different? Those questions can either be present (i.e. who are our customers now) or future: who might our customers be? Keep the tense, present or future, consistent across one session. Don't leave the room until those questions are fully and properly answered. When they are, a sustainable business is born or reborn.
- Hot spot 2: tough decisions. You are going to address what everybody else has been afraid to do: where the money is going to come from. Who do you need to fire? Who do you need to hire? Where will you be based? What are the plans? You have got a whiteboard and all of these are listed, ready to be ticked when they are actioned.
- Hot spot 3: money decisions. Get all the money stuff sorted: a decent profit and loss account, serious cash flow, the necessary pricing calculations, things like guidelines to the sales force on discounting. Ensure invoices are issued promptly and bills chased immediately.

Here's an idea for you...

Do some scenario planning. It's great fun (after the initial 'do we really have to?'). Ask those from your planning group to write a 500-word story of what your company will be like in three years' time. Emphasise that you want detail and narrative rather than bullets – something like 'We will be a player with 60% share of our chosen financial software market: 100% of our transactions will be executed online which will allow us to have a minimal but passionate and dedicated staff...' Ask each of your team to read their stories and then discuss the output. Capture actions for future sessions.

- Hot spot 4: processes and systems. You need great working processes and systems and the more you can automate the better. Who is responsible for a tidy reception area? Quite.
- Hot spot 5: people. You need to develop your best. Recruit more excellent people, brief them, empower them, train them. Get them focused on the new direction of the business.
- Hot spot 6: facts. You need facts, facts about who and what makes the money, which salespeople are worth three of the others, what the markets are doing. Too many businesses, too much of the time, work on guesswork. Not you: knowledge is power.
- Hot spot 7: being brilliant at the basics. Ensure people know how to sell rather than just take orders, how to negotiate rather than just give discounts and how to forecast not just guess; that they know how to manage their time and how to wow the customer. Above all, ensure there is a simple planning round which regularly reviews this list and gives particular attention to innovation...

By the way, without innovation the majority of businesses will die in the New World of Work. This is not hyperbole; what was brilliant rapidly becomes only OK. Innovation is not a choice: it is a necessity. So what is innovation? It's creativity plus action; both are vital and the challenge is that they are almost contradictory skills – free-flow versus discipline; open-ended versus closure; 'off the wall' versus acting within the rules. Address that challenge and yours will be one of the rare truly innovative organisations.

Stage 2: action the 'hot spots'

- Step 1: take the above list and highlight all the areas which you need to address. What needs to be done in your business? Who can action it? And what's the priority? What is the delivery date?
- Step 2: get the management team (perhaps just you, of course) together. Review your thoughts. Get full buy-in. Assign every action to an individual with a report-back date. Set the date for the next meeting when those actions will be reviewed.
- Step 3: keep that cycle going. Every quarter.

If you want to survive, you should carry out the above processes regularly, and think and act differently.

The difficulty lies not in the new ideas, but in escaping from the old ones, which ramify, for those brought up as most of us have been, into every corner of our minds. John Maynard Keynes

189

How did it go?

Q. All of us at the sharp end realise that our customers are deserting us. How do we get our board to see it too?

A. Facts. Facts. Facts. If you are convinced, then you must know something they don't. What is it? Get those facts and share them with impact; your strong emotional feeling is not enough. You could do something like show the decline over a two-year period, or do a statistically valid focus group. Then present your results to the board with conviction and ask for action. Remind them of how plenty of good organisations – from IBM to M&S – have seen a perfectly good business die under them. Sadly it can, and will, happen again.

Q. Where can we get good ideas to stimulate our planning – particularly around reinvention?

A. The key is to do something different. Same old meeting in same old location with same old people equals same old thinking. Changing any one of those elements – perhaps by adding a guest speaker (especially not from your industry or even not from the business world, what about getting someone along to teach you how to juggle?) or holding the meeting in an art gallery – will stimulate fresh thought. Don't forget to capture those resulting thoughts…

46. Start a blog

The world is watching you. Potential future employers are searching for you on the Internet. What does Facebook say about you? Worried? Shades of 1984?

Learn everything you need to know here about turning it all to your advantage.

One fascinating, and at times bizarre, aspect of the New World of Work is how we are now able to talk to the world and connect with each other in an unprecedented manner via clever platforms such as – at the time of writing – Typepad, Facebook, Twitter… As a budding DIY MBAer, what relevance do they all have?

Very high relevance is the answer, and there is good news and bad. The good news is that more than ever you have a way to build the brand and image of you and/or your organisation: quickly and easily, at a modest budget (although, of course, the time commitment can be high). It's a highly targeted and responsive process. And the down side? Well, any network tool such as Facebook needs to be considered carefully –does it reveal to the world what you are happy to reveal to the world? Here's a 'blogger ten' for you.

1. Just to be sure there is no confusion, what is a blog? An online diary, a way of communicating with the world on a regular basis and in a continuous, consistent way. Post by post, day by day. It's targeted, with a definite voice. There are thousands out there, so go and take a look at some. Technorati.com will give you a good route into the blogging world.

2. Blog to talk directly and easily to your customers or potential customers (which, if you are looking for a new job, could be employers) with the voice you choose. This combination of target and voice is remarkably powerful and is certainly unique for its accessibility.

3. You can also blog to build a relationship. Any important relationship – for example, client and supplier – needs regular attention. Blogging is an easy way to do this, an easy way to be there if the client wants you, but not to hassle them if they don't. Blogging gives you an opportunity to inform your clients, to take feedback, and it can be a platform for dealing with problems in an open way.

4. Blog about what is important to you; write as naturally and as easily as you can. Absolutely, definitely, do not be an online brochure with a hard sell. Tell stories, write about incidental stuff; anything which you feel is interesting and will help your client.

Here's an idea for you...

Choose any blogging platform offering a free trial, register and find your way around. At this stage choose mostly default options; don't worry, for example, about design or your biography. Do just check that – at this experimental stage – your blog won't go live until you are ready. Now write; do a post, do an entry on anything: a business issue, an ecology issue, just write on something which you have some passion about. Aim for a couple of hundred words. Proofread it, then preview it. Impressive, huh? Did you enjoy the process? Maybe you are a natural blogger – now it's time to consider going live.

5. Blog regularly to build your readers but also importantly to practise sufficiently that you find out what works for you. Debate rages as to whether you should blog frequently or rarely; just follow your own inclination. If you are serious about it, aim for a couple of entries a week in the early days.

6. Blog with an aim in mind, whether that's to keep your customers informed, to find new customers, to build your brand, to get feedback or to establish yourself as a thought leader in your area.

7. Consider offering some resources on your blog, something to get you talked about. If you are in the T-shirt business, for example, maybe a download of the history of the T-shirt or 'famous T-shirts of the last twenty-five years'. If you are in the organic vegetable business perhaps five recipes guaranteed to work with children. Get creative.

8. Although – as with any community – there are politics and backbiting, the blogging community is generally a generous one. Seek out other bloggers and link to them. They will return the favour and this helps you find your own community more rapidly.

9. Eventually your blog will generate sufficient material that you may well feel you have sufficient for a book. Even if no publisher is interested in it, you could consider self-publishing with many of the online tools now available, such as Lulu.

10. Take a look at my blog. It'll clarify much of the above and give you even more help with your MBA thinking. You'll find it at www.nicholasbate.typepad.com.

I sincerely believe blogging can save America.

John Jay Hooker

How did it go?

Q. *Am I missing out by not blogging?*

A. You are missing out if you don't talk to your customers. If your brand and product are strong enough, word of mouth will always be sufficient, but most of us need a bit of help to augment that process. Once you decide to talk to your community, you have a myriad of possibilities of which blogging is just one. It is however one which is immediate, targeted, cheap and powerful. But it does require commitment and *you* need to do it – you can't outsource it or get your agency to sort it out.

Q. *Where can I learn more about blogging?*

A. Your local online bookstore will have various titles; see what the reviews say about them. Various bloggers blog about blogging (odd as that might seem) and, of course, study the techniques of any bloggers you particularly admire.

47. New World of Work drivers 6: anarchy

Time for one more look at what's going on behind the management and leadership necessary in the New World of Work – a world where power has returned to the people...

And that's bad news for major, arrogant organisations. Good news for you.

Putting it in context

There's a convenient term, the New World of Work, which describes the reality of the working world as it is at the moment. Over the last ten years or so there's been an increasing shift towards 'anarchy' – the ability for individuals to make more of their own decisions, specifically on their careers but also on how they wish to run their lives more generally. There are seven drivers of change which have caused a significant change in the way we work, and anarchy is the sixth of these. Admittedly, increasingly anarchic tendencies have been around for a while; this is simply concerned with the increasing tendency of rigid rules on 'how things should be done' (whether it is for dress codes, publishing music or the arranging of adventure holidays) to disappear.

Anarchy...

Look in any dictionary and you get a definition something along the lines of 'a state of lawlessness, a state of disorder'. And that's exactly what I mean. Of course, the definition normally implies that it's a bad thing, but this is not necessarily so.

Unhappy with your bank? Once upon a time you had to write a letter to the bank manager and wait. And wait. Eventually you would have got a reply based upon a template letter essentially saying 'sorry, but tough'. Now various websites and co-conspirators will help you get your issue sorted and your bank charges repaid. Want to start your own business? Once upon a time you would have found it hard to get funding, or you would have needed a real office, or you would have needed real, expensive staff. Now you can get funds, outsource your key staffing needs, run a budget virtual office, work from a mobile phone and a simple email account.

And there are lots of other examples. Want to sell globally? Once upon a time it was only the big boys who could do that. Now anyone can speak to the world, any time, via the Internet. Want to publish a book? Be a journalist? Once, book publishing was for the few; now, with digital printing, it's a lot easier. And if no one is interested, you can publish your book yourself online and sell it online as well. You want to write and find an audience? Well then, blog. Got an issue? Produce a video; load it on to YouTube. You get the point. Power is in your hands. The question really, is what you are going to do with it.

Here's an idea for you...

Play this mind game for yourself if you run an organisation, or perhaps on behalf of one of your clients. What would it be like if you returned power to the people, if as many rules and regulations as possible were removed? In one or two countries, traffic authorities have experimented with removing traffic lights in towns. What happened? Not mass accidents and increased anguish; no – slower traffic, greater respect for pedestrians and fewer accidents. Done carefully, without removing too much regulation, people become aware of their real responsibilities and take them. So how far could you go? And would you be willing to try?

The implications for organisations

Here are three guidelines for managing anarchy in the organisation:

■ Don't fight it. It's happening and people want it; they want to feel they are running their own lives, they want to make their own decisions and have choices. They don't want to be pushed around, wait or necessarily have the experience or qualifications. Give your customers as much power as they can handle. Their two top desires tend to be choice and the ability to talk to you easily.

■ Make it easy. If customers hate automated call centres, don't say 'tough, they need to get used to it'. Take the automation away instead; you'll have an immediate competitive advantage.

■ Use it as an opportunity to talk and respond to your customers. Get a dialogue going; they will tell you exactly what you need to do to be effective.

The implications for you

Here are three guidelines again:

■ You can do anything. You really can. There are few limits in a world of anarchy.

Undermine their pompous authority, reject their moral standards, make anarchy and disorder your trademarks. Cause as much chaos and disruption as possible but don't let them take you ALIVE. Sid Vicious

- You can't hide. Your job title, your big organisation, your extra qualifications – none of those will protect you any more.
- You're as good as your last gig. It's not your CV that counts; it's the results you deliver. Simple, really!

How did it go?

Q. I'm confused – surely anarchy really is a negative term, without any positive aspects?

A. It has become so. But I'm not necessarily judging the process, determining whether it is exclusively good or bad; I'm simply saying it is a driver in the New World of Work: a fact, whether we approve of it or not. Good? Bad? That depends and it doesn't have to be either; it just exists.

Q. How do I get other people I work with to think positively about this and perhaps adapt more quickly?

A. Strive in your organisation (or with your clients) to begin to remove lots of superfluous regulations and rules. They tend to accumulate and 'layer' as time goes on, remember. Simplify, simplify, simplify, then simplify some more and encourage individuals to take responsibility for their actions and not just 'blame the management'.

48. Inspiration

Occasionally, just occasionally, the world of work will get you down. This will get you inspired again – great thinking from the world's greatest thinkers: all in one place.

And there's a plus: wisdom in a nutshell for your business.

Sometimes, just sometimes, it can all get too much. Too many business models, too many ways of differentiation, of adding value. Another strategic thinker, another business model. We can begin to lose the wood for the trees. Well, not on this MBA course! Read and re-read the thoughts of the following well-known people: firstly, they inspire; secondly, they encapsulate great wisdom and, thirdly, they do both of those quickly.

Dream as if you will live forever. Live as if you will die today. James Dean
In business: think big, think long term. Have a vision. But be excellent today.
Personally: act on your vision, but live in the moment.

Follow your bliss. Joseph Campbell
In business: build a business you truly, passionately believe in.
Personally: do what you love, nothing less.

Talent is in choices. Robert De Niro
In business: nothing is easy, but do choose; don't just react.
Personally: it's down to you. Choose.

You are the storyteller of your own life and you can create your own legend – or not. Isabel Allende
In business: decide to be an awe-inspiring organisation.
Personally: decide to be your own legend.

Begin it! Goethe
In business: turn decisions into actions.
Personally: nothing happens until you start.

It is not the strongest of the species that survive nor the most intelligent, but the one most responsive to change. Charles Darwin
In business: stay lean and mean and fast, however big you get.
Personally: break patterns; stay flexible.

Love the dip, Love the plateau. George Leonard
In business: things will go wrong; it's how you respond which is the important point.
Personally: getting stuck and making mistakes are part of the learning process.

You must be the change you wish to see in the world. Gandhi
In business: don't complain about lack of integrity in the business world; have integrity instead.
Personally: be brilliant in all you do.

Here's an idea for you...

Who are your greatest thought leaders? Who inspires you? Obviously in business, but perhaps in others areas too, such as the arts, cooking, architecture? Take a few of your business cards and put a line through the front so you don't accidentally give them out. Then capture a quote from your inspirer on the blank side. Build up a small set of these and carry them in your briefcase or bag. When you are on your way to a tough meeting, read them. Getting lost in a strategy planning meeting? Read them. Losing market share? Definitely read them. Start writing those cards now.

Whatever you do, do it with passion. Carlos Castaneda
In business: enthuse every part of your business to make excellence the minimum standard.
Personally: do it with passion or pack it in.

Forget to remember the stuff you don't need any more. Richard Bandler
In business: history is, well, history. Think of the future.
Personally: OK, so you learned something; now move on.

And in the end, the love you take is equal to the love you make. Paul McCartney
In business: invest in your clients and partners and staff.
Personally: every relationship is an investment: invest well

Those who never take risks can only see other people's failures. Paulo Coelho
In business: grab the opportunities.
Personally: set stretching goals and execute them.

Don't be trapped by dogma – living with the results of other people's thinking. Steve Jobs
In business: there is absolutely no box which you cannot think beyond.
Personally: break patterns which hold you back.

There is no way to happiness. Happiness is the way. The Dalai Lama
In business: enjoy the business-development journey.
Personally: enjoy the quest.

Use the quotations in several ways.

■ To unlock your thinking. (For example, 'If we knew this was all about the correct decision, what's the question?' That's the De Niro.)

■ As background inspiration. ('What's the dogma we are assuming in this market?' – using the Steve Jobs quote.)

■ As a step change. ('What would we need to do if everybody in this organisation worked with passion?' – Castaneda's…)

■ For your daily focus ('What's this week's plateau and how can I push through it?' inspired by George Leonard.)

No man was ever great without divine inspiration. Cicero

How did it go?

Q. *I really like the idea of building up my own set of inspirational quote cards, but where can I find good quotes?*

A. The best source is undoubtedly your own reading, whether a business book or not. If you're reading non-fiction always have a notebook to hand and then, whenever a phrase or sentence inspires or amuses you, jot it down. Sometimes there'll be a great idea or concept – rather than write it all out, try and find a phrase or sentence which truly captures it. In addition to your own search – which is undoubtedly the best way to do it – the Internet has many sites which collect quotations and additionally categorise them. These are, of course, a great resource but they do tend to be the 'classic' quotes (nothing wrong with those, mind) and nothing is quite as fresh and immediate as the ones you created yourself.

Q. *How do I use the quotes to actually create change and action, rather than just have a general feeling of inspiration and feeling good?*

A. Great question: let's answer it practically. Take the Gandhi quote from the list above. Great quote? Yes, definitely. Inspirational? Yes! So what do you do with it? Well, let's say many managers are complaining that their teams are failing to offer excellent customer service. The first place to start is to brainstorm how, as managers, they can offer their own staff excellent service – treating them with respect, keeping them informed, delivering on promises. It works, and does so profoundly. Keep that quotation close and act on it.

49. New World of Work drivers 7: adrenaline

Here's another detailed look at the backdrop to the management and leadership needed in the New World of Work. Drivers 1 to 6 stack up to one big driver: fear...

How to manage the fear of change and turbulence in business and markets.

The context

The term 'New World of Work' is a label for the world of work as it is right now. This world came into existence perhaps ten years ago with an increasing tendency towards many things, including 'adrenaline' – the fear of change. It's not at all the same as the Old World of Work. There are seven drivers of change which have caused a significant alteration in the way we work, moving it away from the Old World of Work and, of course, 'adrenaline' in this sense has been around for some time. However, the increasing tendency for people to feel anxious about their long-term career is comparatively new.

Let's go over the other six drivers briefly, checking out what they are and what their implications are, both for individuals and for organisations.

- Driver 1: acceleration. This is the increasing rate of change; not so much change itself which has clearly always been with us, but the actual rate of that change. It tends to encourage an alarming push for efficiency (doings things

Here's an idea for you...

What's something which makes you a little anxious or very scared, in a business setting? Presentations come to mind for many, of course. Perhaps tackling difficult people or chasing for late payments or… You've got a few; everyone has. Whatever it is, I want you to do it, I want you to tackle that fear, because once you have you will feel so good. That presentation, or picking up the phone and chasing that person who has been holding back your overdue payment – do it now.

right) rather than effectiveness (doing the right things) in organisations. This can make for a stressful environment. The best personal strategy is to slow down to the speed of thought.

- Driver 2: automation. This is the move to replace any possible process with a chip; to go high tech. All well and good, but humans tend to be at their best when handled in a high-touch environment. The push towards the former can remove the soul from an organisation as well as creating a political environment for the individual. Here the best personal strategy is to use the best of high tech, but stay high touch.

- Driver 3: alternative shores. There is always somewhere cheaper in the world, and with the advent of the Internet and the global market 'alternative shoring' is now a valid possibility. The key message for everyone is don't become a commodity; build your personal brand – otherwise you are likely to be replaced.

- Driver 4: abundance. So much choice, in everything from personal finance to vegetables. How do you cope? Well, as both organisations and individuals the answer is to raise standards and make excellence your minimum choice. There are never enough excellent people around the place.

- Driver 5: ambiguity. The death of long-term planning; the unreliability of planning. For the organisation this means staying lean and mean in thinking and responsiveness. For the individual? Think like an entrepreneur: you run your own business, now.

- Driver 6: anarchy. Power is back with the people, the Internet, rising qualifications, one market… Whatever the reasons, big is no longer powerful. Listen to the people and they will do business with you; ignore them and they will bring you down.

Add up (or more realistically, multiply) the above factors and find the product/sum. And what do you get? Searing adrenaline, that's what. An intense fear of what's next and of what you do with it.

Adrenaline: fear

For you as an individual, this will be your biggest barrier. You must learn to manage fear as an individual and hence as an organisation. Left as a raw emotion this fear is debilitating and will stop both you and your employees – and hence your organisation – being as effective as possible. In these circumstances people will take an easy choice perhaps over the right choice, the short-term escape perhaps over the long-term strategic path and opt for 10% of personal potential rather than 110%. What's to be done? Here are five suggestions.

Managing fear

1. Most fear is mindset. Fear is there for a reason, whether that's battling with bears or leaping chasms – but in the day-to-day business world it can be considered just a 'checking' emotion.
2. No failure, only feedback. It's literally how you look at it. Had a bad quarter's results? So, what are you going to do about it?
3. Feel the fear and do it anyway: Susan Jeffer's great quote. Feel it, notice it, do it – anyway.
4. Chase challenge, not comfort. It's actually appropriate fear and challenge which gives everyone the necessary buzz, not comfort.
5. Don't blame the kids. They don't want you to have no excitement, to become boring. Don't blame them: get on with it.

The thing I fear is fear itself.

Michel de Montaigne, *Essais*

How did it go?

Q. Can you give me any practical tips when I feel fearful?

A. Well, there are several good ones; here are a couple – and a reminder – I've found effective. In the first place, take a steady walk. This forces the body to pick up a natural rhythm and stabilise again. Then don't allow your mind to focus on what is going on; do this by just saying a junk word, such as 'next, next, next' until your mind clears the worry. Finally, you can't say to yourself 'don't worry', because you just worry more!

Q. How do I get others to think like this and move more quickly when we're under pressure?

A. Run some training and/or workshops. Get people to realise that change will be the norm, that it is not unusual to feel anxious, but that there are practical ways of managing it. Above all, keep people informed. No news is rarely good news in times of change.

50. More than a team player: a networker

Of course you know about teamwork, but what about the extended team? The network? Networking isn't just jargon; it's an essential part of your MBA.

Here's how to choose, manage and profit from your network.

What is a network?

Your network is a collection of individuals who have in common the fact that you know them all through business (one or two might be social friends, too), you enjoy their company and they have skills and/or contacts which may well be useful to you at some stage. Equally you have something to offer them, and you are all interested in becoming more effective and supporting each other. A great network is based – as you'll see – on abundance thinking, not manipulation.

What's the big deal?

Business is tough enough; why not increase every possible chance you can to be more successful? An easy one is to make more use of the great people you meet on a regular basis, all of the time. Your network – well managed – can get you business, get you jobs, find you staff, warn you about scams, help you with great tips… so how do you make a successful network?

Here's an idea for you...

When you meet people, make an effort to be interested in them; find out what they do. Ask if you can stay in touch and add them to your network. They may become an important player, they may not; at this stage it doesn't matter. What does matter is that it is very easy to meet great potential people for your network but, through lack of attention, lack of effort or too much politeness (or even fear), you lose them. Is it pushy to keep in contact? No, only if you act that way. Do it with politeness and most people will be fine about it.

Stage 1: capture your network

This is one of those enjoyable pencil and paper exercises. Grab those. If you can, finding a sheet from a flipchart pad would be great; if not, take a minute or two to stick four A4 sheets together to make an A3 sheet (that's a large rectangle). Right – here's the enjoyable and intriguing part. Keep the writing small; if you can, be patient and print. Put your name in the centre, then draw radiating lines to the names of people you know. This will probability grow organically, with the people with the closest relationships and whom you know best being most adjacent to your own name. Keep thinking and capturing until you feel you have your network – everybody you know – documented. Now add the name of any person that someone on your network knows and whom you would also like to get to know. Now add the names of anybody you are aware of that you would like to get to know, and add them to your network.

Stage 2: formalise your network

Choose a pre-packed networking tool – there are many – or simply type your contacts into a database, recording their names accurately with all the contact details you have. Add a personal note to all of them; you may remember them at the moment, but maybe not in a year's time. So add a personal note such as 'chatted to him for about an hour at Toronto airport while delayed in snowstorm, works at Starbucks, was worried about his daughter's choice of university'. Finally create a prompt which will encourage you to contact the person concerned and decide the level of frequency of contact. I suggest either once a month, once a quarter or twice a year.

Stage 3: ignite your network

Start working through your contacts. Some, of course, you will currently be working with but with the others look for opportunities to contact them, to help them and to support them. For those with whom you have – as yet – had no direct contact, but where you would like to be able to initiate conversation, write being honest: 'I recently read your book and have been fascinated by your blog and I thought the following might be of interest to you…'

Stage 4: be abundant

The key to getting your network to work is to just help and not look for any immediate return. Think 'New Age' if you wish and call it karma; be scientific and call it Newton III. Either way, what goes about does (sometimes after a very long route, agreed) tend to come back. And that's the fun. Be abundant and send all sorts of things: ideas, clippings, links, details of a book you've read, a contact, a postcard from a fascinating place, details of a job, a request to tender for business – whatever.

Business opportunities are like buses, there's always another one coming. Richard Branson

How did it go?

Q. Mmm. Karma? Newton III? I'm sorry, but I have several friends who have built networks and say they have got nothing out of the whole process. Isn't it simply a load of old bullshit?

A. May I be so bold as to suggest that your friends probably hadn't followed the above guidelines? If you do persevere, if you do intend to help others, if you do give it time, then your network will take off. But you do have to be patient.

Q. What about all the social network systems which are available online?

A. Try them and if they work for you, fine. The big danger (and this is rapidly now becoming a huge problem) is the time needed to maintain them and the expectations that people set up with each other. That's why I prefer my own 'home-made' simple system and tend to stay clear of the commercial ones. As with most things, it's the principle which is crucial, not the mechanics.

51. The answer sheet

You found that quickly, didn't you? Something else you don't get on a course: the complete answer sheet!

Here it is in easy steps: what you need to do to thrive in the New World of Work; how to get your MBA thinking to work for you.

Recognise it

Recognise that there is a 'New World of Work': a world in which in every market possesses its own tipping point, a point at which markets irrevocably change and are never the same again. Banking (no more bank managers), retail (stores within stores), leisure (the exotic experience): you name it, the market is experiencing its tipping point. Recognise that it is happening to your own market. Do you know what it is?

Stay on top of it

Create a team who meet once a month to observe, track and identify the changes in your market. A cross-organisation team who turn thoughts and observations ('mmm – that's interesting!') into decisions ('let's get out of that market') and decisions into actions ('let's notify all customers that we will only support that product for a further eighteen months').

Here's an idea for you...

Answer the following questions at speed (and you can answer on behalf of one of your clients if you wish). What is your business about? What is the next strategic direction for your business? What are four steps you would need to implement to ensure that strategic direction? What is the biggest blocker to your potential success? How can you overcome it? What must be done to ensure your survival in the New World of Work? Who 'owns' those actions? What are you going to do immediately to get this all started?

Get a plan

Ensure your organisation has a plan. It's on a wall in the action room; it's highly visible. It's clear what has been done and what needs to be done. On the personal level, ensure you have a plan for your career: what will you be doing in three years' time and how will you get there? Ensure every one of your employees has a plan, too; help them realise their dreams. Sure, one or two may leave but they will be eternally grateful to you. The rest will step up from 12% output to 87%.

Work that plan

Turn that plan into actions with milestones and owners. Hold the owners accountable for the actions, particularly the delivery milestones.

Reinvent

Regularly get together and brainstorm and ask these questions: 'How can we be better – how can we be even better – than we are currently? What will stop us? Who can help us? What are we missing which with hindsight would seem so obvious?' Allow time for the best thinking. Walk, take breaks and get off site. Have a facilitator; manage the flipcharts and yellow stickies. Record everything.

Be brilliant at the basics

Ensure sales are selling, strategic marketing are strategically marketing and accounts are doing the accounts and you are leading. Get the basics done and done properly. Identify any blockers to execution of the basics and remove them.

Be innovative

Innovation is creativity plus action – challengingly different skills. Ensure your staff know how to create, but also how to implement.

Inspire people

Your job as a leader is to ensure that people are the best version of themselves; you do that by inspiring them.

Use challenge to create comfort

Human beings are at their best when they are reaching out to an appropriate goal. Create and articulate clear achievable goals which stretch; reward success, understand and learn from failure.

Use high tech, but stay high touch

Be efficient with what needs efficiency – things such as the processing of emails, the creation of proposal templates. Be effective with what needs effectiveness – such as writing that email or playing with your children. Don't confuse 'getting stuff done' with getting the right stuff done.

Do it with passion or pack it in.

It's obvious, really: why would you want to do anything for more than a day or two if you have no passion for it? Quite. Look for the intrinsic worth in what you do. Get passionate. But if you can't, find what does turn you on and get into it.

Keep learning

You started your own MBA. Think how much it has helped you; don't stop now. Continue to read and develop, set up a learning team, book yourself on to some courses, buy some time from a consultant. Do whatever it takes to be an avid learner and stay ahead of the crowd. Stay a lifelong learner.

It is not the strongest of the species that survives, nor the most intelligent, but the one most responsive to change. Charles Darwin

How did it go?

Q. Your list is a great list, but there's a lot on it. Where on earth do I start?

A. The most important thing is to start: it would be a rare organisation who could do everything, but the organisations which are likely to survive are those who do something. Remember the useful Pareto Principle or the 80/20 rule, which reminds us that 20% of focused attention can give a dramatic 80% of results. Choose anything from that list and work on it.

Q. I'm still unsure about this New World of Work concept and whether it's really such a step change. Surely change is continuous?

A. Yes, change is continuous – but the graph, the line, is not smooth. There are steps in it: the advent of the computer in the office was a step change, for instance, and the advent of the PC on the desk was a huge step change. Those step changes are now appearing at increasingly frequent intervals. There have been sufficient in most markets to make them totally unrecognisable when compared to what they were before. Contrast the bank of twenty-five years ago (short opening hours, banking halls, the bank is king) with that of today (open 24–7 via the Internet, the customer is king, virtual locations) and you'll see what I mean.

52. Beyond the MBA

So: what's next? You've done brilliantly. How do you keep the momentum going? How do you stay top of your field?

And the best news? No final exams to sweat about: you've passed!

Doing your own instant MBA has taught you a lot. It has got you thinking, thinking differently, and you have realised that more than ever you must stay different, stay distinct. But how do you do that now that you have finished this basic curriculum? Read on.

Keep reading
You've discovered the amazing resource of blogs. Always read a few every day: the latest posts, links and downloads, read and follow them up with book references. Always have a book on the go; it really does not matter if it takes you a whole year to read it. Keep the stimulation going.

Keep listening
Download podcasts, get audio-CD versions of business books. Listen in to the business news in the morning, especially whist driving or on the train; always have something useful which you are listening to. It's such an easy and time-effective way to stay at your best.

Here's an idea for you...

Get a wall planner (if it's the 'wrong' time of year, you can get undated ones); you need twelve months, but eighteen would be great. They normally have sticky symbols that come with them; if not, make your own. On the sticky write down the things you would like to do to continue your self-development path in order to keep you ahead of the game. They can be general ('read more') or specific ('read *The Long Tail*'). Brainstorm deeply (offer to do a case study for a client free) and wide (maybe sign up for a cookery class by a top chef).

Keep thinking

Challenge yourself to be creative ('How could we do this given that we don't have any budget?'), be innovative ('What would be the fresh way to address this market?'), be reflective ('Just how good are we?'). Challenge yourself to be different.

Keep debating

Set up a learning team of three. Meet once a month for an hour to debate and to challenge each other. Get good at disagreeing without losing the relationship. Change the team once a year. If you work for a large employer, try and get different people into the team from different organisations.

Keep being challenged

Work hard at ideas which stretch you. Try and understand thought leaders with whom you fundamentally disagree. If you are a 'people person', work at the numbers; if you are a techie, work at the emotional intelligence, the people stuff.

Keep implementing

Don't just talk about stuff – actually do it. 'Let's get more strategic' – OK, how? 'We need to price better' – OK, how?

Keep doing

Experiment. Do some work for some clients for free to gain experience. Learn, learn, learn…

Keep investing

Create your learning budget. Use it for courses, books, coaching. And keep increasing it.

Keep breaking patterns

You don't believe in online advertising? Maybe that's exactly why you should try it. You think focus groups are biased? Maybe that's exactly why you should run one…

Keep remembering that you run your own business

Whether you really are self-employed and a one-man band, a small, red-hot consultancy or a worker in a large organisation, ensure that your mindset is that of someone who runs their own thing: who has a strategic plan, has an investment budget and is determined to be an excellent return on investment rather than a hefty cost centre.

Keep remembering that you are only as good as your last gig

That's what people look at. 'Oh, the last album wasn't that great. Not sure about his last book… Did you go to his last workshop? Terrible, wasn't it?'

Keep trying

Raise your standards, stay focused, stay flexible. Make excellence your minimum standard.

Keep leading

Be determined to be the best in your niche. The best gets all the rewards; the word of mouth, the profit, the key customers, the challenge – and the fun. So be the best in your particular niche.

Have you invested as much this year in your career as in your car? Molly Sargent, consultant and trainer

How did it go?

Q. Should I get more 'recognised' qualifications now?

A. I guess there are two things to consider here, one a little more philosophical than the other. Firstly, be confident in your own 'unrecognised' leanings. Not all learning comes with a pass or an accreditation or a qualification. And recognise that this is, well, OK. If we only chase after qualifications which are formalised we can miss out on some of the very best learning in life. Attending a t'ai chi class every week at the local college may teach you a lot more about strategy than your Open University distance-learning MBA ever did, for instance. Then once you have created your own MBA, consider more vocational training – if people skills are your big interest, for example, you might do a Myers–Briggs course.

Q. Should I now do an MBA 'for real'?

A. Maybe, maybe not! You've got so much of the necessary learning done already, so why do that? Well, of course, it formalises your learning. Having done all this work you will find 'the real thing' a whole lot easier and be able to enjoy more of the projects and networking. You'll know which electives/modules you really want to do. On the other hand, think how you could use the money – maybe as a starting payment on your own business, maybe to send yourself on vocational courses at regular intervals, maybe to take six months' sabbatical and travel, maybe to work part-time while you write the novel. These options may well be more interesting, more worthwhile and ultimately teach you more than a formal full-time, part-time or distance-learning MBA. If there is one thing your own MBA has taught you, it's this: be different. So – be different! Good luck!

Resources

Here it is: but it's different. Books on how to be a revolutionary, make friends with anyone and still manage a project brilliantly. Plus the best blogs. This is a time where you need ideas, so start immersing yourself in them – now. You'll love this list.

Personal effectiveness and making stuff happen

The Effective Executive, Peter Drucker (2006 edition)
Calm, balanced writing by the guru's guru. Concentrates more on mindset and 'right thinking' rather than too many complex systems which – in my view – is the only true route to long-term effectiveness.

Ready for Anything, David Allen (2004)
The 'getting things done guy', but a more philosophical book. An excellent read and in simple standalone sections so it can be read in short time periods such as morning commutes. Good clear insights on the productivity challenges which face all of us.

Bit Literacy, Mark Hurst (2007)
Not enough has been written about time management in the Internet age and how to cope with the advent of email. This great book tackles the issue head on; the author has also produced a simple online system.

Rules for Radicals, Saul Alinsky (1989 reissue)
I promised you some very different reads – this is one. An inspiring book of how to create change. Wide ranging and practical, it will give you the courage to do what needs to be done.

Peopleware, Tom Demarco (1999, second edition)
He is the best writer on project management. No, don't be put off. You need to understand this topic and after reading this book you will enjoy the subject, no doubt about it.

Simple, practical psychology
How to Win Friends and Influence People, Dale Carnegie (1936!)
This is, of course, the classic book and it has never really been bettered. Settle down to an enjoyable read.

Made to Stick, Chip and Dan Heath (2007)
A fun book on how to get your ideas to spread and to stick.

On being an entrepreneur
The 4-Hour Work Week, Timothy Ferris (2007)
This book caused a bit of a storm on first release and very much polarised its audience. But by reading carefully and extracting what can work for you, it can really 'flip' the way you look at the world of work.

The Art of the Start, Guy Kawasaki (2004)
This is a man who knows what he is talking about, having been in at the start of Apple and many subsequent start-ups.

Both Ferris and Kawasaki have blogs.

Leadership and management

The Practice of Management, Peter Drucker (originally 1954; go for the latest edition)
Ignore the rest, go straight to the best. Read and absorb and practise.

Strategy

Competitive Strategy, Michael Porter (2004 edition)
It's a hefty, academic tome, but it is the original, the masterpiece.

Leading the Revolution, Gary Hamel (2002, second edition)
A refreshingly heretical counterpoint to Porter.

In Search of Excellence, Tom Peters (1982)
The other classic in the field. Read it. Not so much has changed and despite Peters' critics, that's not a bad record for a book which is this old.

The Internet

The Long Tail, Chris Anderson (2006)
If you think you understand the Internet, read this book and be introduced to a fascinating world. Discover also how the book came out of his blog and how the Long Tail can be applied to many different areas in life. But first – discover what it is.

Numbers

36-Hour Course in Finance for Non-Financial Managers, Robert Cooke (2004, second edition)
Consistently highly rated, it's all you need; clear and precise.

Life

The War of Art, Steven Pressfield (2003)
A magnificent book. Pressfield is usually a historical novelist, but thank goodness he wrote this book. It's for all of us aspiring artists who are trying to release our art, be that literally art or a book or a start-up or… He will overcome your blockers. Read it. Soon.

Man's Search for Meaning, Victor Frankl (2000 edition)
Things will never be the same after reading this book. Another one to read – today.

Blogs

Start building your collection of blogs which you regularly peruse. Start with Seth Godin and Tom Peters; the latter has an extensive 'blog roll' which will allow you to rapidly find other blogs which you enjoy.

Plus, consider
- Reading biographies of historical figures (Churchill, Thatcher, Kennedy), or of business leaders (Gates).
- Stretching your musical tastes.
- Reading more fiction.
- Reading the classics.

Learn more about your thought leaders

Michael Porter

Competitive Strategy (1980), his seminal work, now in its sixty-third imprint.
His other main works are:
Competitive Advantage (1985)
The Competitive Advantage of Nations (1990)
Can Japan Compete? (1999)

Gary Hamel

Competing for the Future (1996)
Leading the Revolution (2002)
The Future of Management (2007)

Unfortunately, neither Porter nor Hamel has a blog but if you search the Internet you will discover many relevant articles, summaries of conferences written by bloggers and critiques of their work. These will all help deepen your understanding of ideas which are fundamental to the healthy operation of a business.

Tom Peters

Start with his blog at www.tompeters.com. Then dip into these as appropriate (particularly the first four):
In Search of Excellence (1982)
The Tom Peters Seminar: Crazy Times Call for Crazy Organizations (1993)
The Brand You 50, The Project 50 and The Professional Service Firm 50 (1999)
Re-imagine! Business Excellence in a Disruptive Age (2003)
A Passion for Excellence (1985)
Thriving on Chaos (1987)

Liberation Management (1992)

The Pursuit of WOW! (1994)

The Circle of Innovation: You Can't Shrink Your Way to Greatness (1997)

Talent (2005)

Leadership (2005)

Design (2005)

Trends (2005)

Peter Drucker

The Practice of Management (1954) is his seminal work.

Check these out, too:

The Effective Executive (1966)

Managing in Turbulent Times (1980)

The Essential Drucker: The Best of Sixty Years of Peter Drucker's Essential Writings on Management (2001)

The Daily Drucker: 366 Days of Insight and Motivation for Getting the Right Things Done (2004)

Clearly, he does not have a blog but if you go online you will find an abundance of relevant articles and critiques of his work. These will all help deepen your understanding of the thinking of 'the father of modern management'.

Daniel Goleman

Start with his blog at www.danielgoleman.info/blog/ and then dip into these as appropriate (the first three are the key ones):

Emotional Intelligence: Why It Can Matter More Than IQ (1996)

Primal Leadership: The Hidden Driver of Great Performance (2001)

The Emotionally Intelligent Workplace (2001)

Social Intelligence: The New Science of Social Relationships (2006)

Harvard Business Review, 'What Makes a Leader?' (1998)

Working with Emotional Intelligence (1998)

Healing Emotions: Conversations with the Dalai Lama on Mindfulness, Emotions, and Health (1997)

The Meditative Mind (1988).

Vital Lies, Simple Truths: The Psychology of Self Deception (1985)

Jim Collins

Start with his excellent website at www.jimcollins.com. Then dip into these as appropriate (especially the first two):

Built to Last (with Jerry I. Porras) (1994)

Good to Great: Why Some Companies Make the Leap… And Others Don't (2001)

Beyond Entrepreneurship: Turning Your Business into an Enduring Great Company (with William C. Lazier) (1995)

Good to Great and the Social Sectors (2005)

And more...

Consider making contact with your local business school and see if any of the lecturers have a particular Good to Great/Built to Last/Level 5 Leadership thing and would be interested in possibly working in partnership with you. They would get some 'real world' data for their research/next book; you would get some practical advice on how to implement the ideas.

And, remember, many of the books you read (and certainly most on the above list) will contain a reading list. A good author's recommended list is gold dust. It's where they reveal where their ideas came from and how their concepts to date have been formed. Add their books to your book-buying or borrowing wish-list.

When you meet someone you admire in business, ask them about the books which have most influenced them, fiction as well as non-fiction. Over time you'll hear some repeated titles – *The Road Less Travelled* by M. Scott Peck, for example (yes, add it to your list) – make sure you read them. You'll also discover some odd, eclectic ones; definitely read those, too.

The end...

Or is it a new beginning?

We hope that these ideas will have helped you get all fired up and ready for business success. Whether you're using the ideas to help you decide if an MBA is for you or to put you on the fast-track to career success you should be feeling more confident about your career prospects and be buzzing with new ideas – maybe you're even ready for that promotion.

So why not let us know about it? Tell us how you got on. What did it for you – which ideas really made a difference to your thinking, performance or earnings? Maybe you've got some tips of your own that you'd like to share. And if you liked this book you may find we have even more brilliant ideas that could help change other areas of your life for the better.

You'll find the Infinite Ideas crew waiting for you online at www.infideas.com.

Or if you prefer to write, then send your letters to:
Instant MBA
Infinite Ideas Ltd
36 St Giles, Oxford, OX1 3LD, United Kingdom

We want to know what you think, because we're all working on making our lives better too. Give us your feedback and you could win a copy of another **52 Brilliant Ideas** book of your choice. Or maybe get a crack at writing your own.

Good luck. Be brilliant.

Offer one

Cash in your ideas

We hope you enjoy this book. We hope it inspires, amuses, educates and entertains you. But we don't assume that you're a novice, or that this is the first book that you've bought on the subject. You've got ideas of your own. Maybe our author has missed an idea that you use successfully. If so, why not send it to yourauthormissedatrick@infideas.com, and if we like it we'll post it on our bulletin board. Better still, if your idea makes it into print we'll send you four books of your choice or the cash equivalent. You'll be fully credited so that everyone knows you've had another Brilliant Idea.

Offer two

How could you refuse?

Amazing discounts on bulk quantities of Infinite Ideas books are available to corporations, professional associations and other organisations.

For details call us on:
+44 (0)1865 514888
Fax: +44 (0)1865 514777
or email: info@infideas.com

Where it's at...

THE LEARNING CENTRE
HAMMERSMITH AND WEST
LONDON COLLEGE
GLIDDON ROAD
LONDON W14 9BL